VISIO 2000
Visual Insight

David N. Plotkin

CORIOLIS™

The Coriolis Group, LLC
14455 North Hayden Road, Suite 220
Scottsdale, Arizona 85260

480/483-0192
FAX: 480/483-0193
http://www.coriolis.com

Library of Congress Cataloging-In-Publication Data
Plotkin, David.
Visio 2000 visual insight/ by David Plotkin.
    p. cm
ISBN 1-57610-532-6
    1. Mechanical drawing. 2. Visio. I. Title.
T353.P637   2000
604.2'0285'5369--dc21   99-054513
                                CIP

President, CEO
Keith Weiskamp

Publisher
Steve Sayre

Marketing Specialist
Beth Kohler

Project Editor
Melissa D. Olson

Technical Reviewer
Jon McFarland

Production Coordinator
Meg E. Turecek

Cover Designer
Jody Winkler

Layout Designer
April Nielsen

Printed in the United States of America
10 9 8 7 6 5 4 3 2 1

As with most other married authors, this book is dedicated to my wife and partner, Marisa. She provided me the freedom to spend the time necessary to do a good job on this book, my first in a long while.

❧

About The Author

As a senior data administrator for Longs Drug Stores, **David N. Plotkin** designs and models complex computer systems. He has used Visio since version 1, and he has been convinced that a book about Visio has been needed for quite some time. He has written two books about computer software and contributed chapters for many more. He is married to Marisa, an attorney who writes children's books. He is an avid bicyclist, and he believes that deadlines should *never* get in the way of exercising.

Acknowledgments

I've always wanted to write this section as, "Nobody. I did it all myself." But that wouldn't be true or fair. Lots of people helped bring this book to print. Chief among them was Rich Adolf of Waggener-Edstrom (Visio's PR firm), who kept me up-to-date on releases and information, and rousted the Visio folks when the final version wouldn't install over the beta. Thanks also to Brady Brewer and Samantha Lima-Campos of Visio Corporation, who answered many questions and made sure I got what I needed. Mariann Barsolo was the acquisitions editor at The Coriolis Group, and she was a delight to work with, even if I did overwhelm her by turning in the manuscript early.

Contents At A Glance

Table Of Contents

Introduction

Graphical diagrams, such as flow charts, organization charts, floor plans, decision trees, and the like, are usually difficult to build and *boring*. But it doesn't have to be that way. Visio 2000 combines the ease of click-and-drag with powerful formatting features to make it easy and fun to build eye-catching diagrams. If you need to build diagrams to communicate information (and incidentally, impress your audience with your expertise), this book will get you started quickly. Without overwhelming you with unnecessarily detailed explanations, you can learn to use the tool and become productive fast. The proven technique of explaining with text and showing with pictures will make it possible for you to create diagrams in Visio almost immediately.

What Is In The Book

This book starts by introducing the software and telling you how to navigate in Visio 2000. Then, it tells you how to build a simple diagram using the shapes that Visio provides and the templates (drawing types) that come with the software package. But you can do far more, including changing the color, fill, shadow, line type, and font of shapes and connecting lines, and this book covers all your options. I'll tell you how to attach your own special properties to shapes and how to use Visio's special functions to create your own shapes and templates. You'll need to know this information in order to create diagrams that stand out from the crowd. Finally, you'll build a series of relatively complex projects to use the skills you have learned. These projects will help you see how the information you read earlier in the book can be used to perform useful work (which is, after all, what we get paid for).

Most books are organized logically from front to back, and this one is no exception. Each chapter covers a topic that is fairly independent of the other chapters, but the projects presented in the last four chapters build on the techniques and examples presented earlier in the book. So, unless you have used Visio before, it is probably best to read the book straight through and try the examples and projects in the order they are presented. Here are highlights from each chapter:

- *Chapter 1*—Explains the screen elements, windows, and how to get help.
- *Chapter 2*—Tells you how to configure the program's toolbars, menus, and general options.
- *Chapter 3*—Leads you through creating your first diagram by using Visio templates and also starting from a blank slate. You learn how to open multiple groups of shapes (called *stencils*). Most importantly, this chapter teaches you how to drag shapes onto the drawing surface, connect them using lines, and add text to a diagram.

- *Chapter 4*—Shows you how to change the properties of a page, add pages to a diagram, and make effective use of color. It also teaches you how to use some of the more advanced drawing tools, including snap and grid, rulers, zoom, and headers and footers.

- *Chapter 5*—Introduces you to changing shape and line properties, as well as grouping shapes together, stacking them on the page, and flipping and rotating shapes.

- *Chapter 6*—Shows you how to change text and paragraph properties, such as the font, size, indent, angle, and color. You also learn how to spell check your text.

- *Chapter 7*—Builds on the lessons in Chapter 5, giving you more powerful tools for editing shapes. You will learn to attach custom properties to a shape; create and apply styles to shapes, lines, and text; and merge shapes to create new shapes. This chapter also covers working with clip art in a Visio diagram, and creating and attaching hyperlinks to shapes.

- *Chapter 8*—Tells you how to create your own Visio tools, such as master shapes (the shapes that appear in the stencils) and your own stencils. This chapter also shows you how to create your own templates (types of diagrams).

- *Chapter 9*—Shows you how to control the behavior of shapes by creating multiple layers in a diagram, specifying the properties of a layer, and assigning shapes to various layers.

- *Chapter 10*—Is the first of the four project chapters. In this chapter, you lay out furniture in a room, including specifying the room dimensions and properties, such as light switches, closets, windows, and electrical outlets.

- *Chapter 11*—Uses a special Visio template to walk you through creating an organization chart from a spreadsheet. After you create the org chart, you can reformat how the data is displayed.

- *Chapter 12*—Uses a wizard to create a timeline for buying and installing the furniture you laid out in Chapter 10. You learn to create and edit tasks, assign durations and resources, and track progress.

- *Chapter 13*—Shows you how to use Visio with other applications. For example, you can embed a Visio diagram in a word processing document, and even edit the Visio diagram right from your Word processor.

Part I
Techniques And Tasks

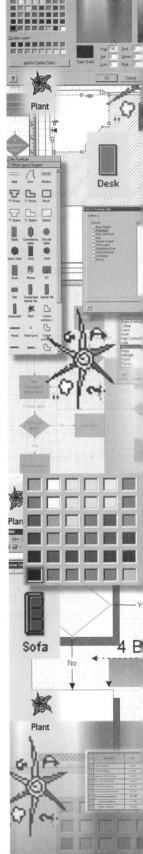

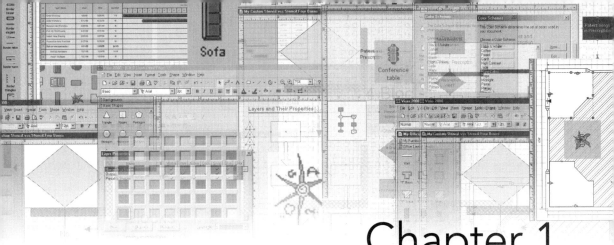

Chapter 1
Navigating In Visio

- View the main screen elements

- Use the buttons in the toolbars

- Add windows to the screen

- Get shape help

- Get template help

Getting Started

This chapter introduces you to Visio's screen elements and basic tools. In addition to "standard" Windows features, such as menus and toolbars, Visio 2000 provides special windows that provide information about the diagrams you are working on. In addition, Visio 2000 doesn't leave you on your own if you need help figuring something out. The application provides standard Windows Help, as well as concise descriptions for diagram and stencil types.

Viewing The Main Screen Elements

Visio 2000 is powerful tool for creating many kinds of diagrams, including block diagrams, flowcharts, furniture layouts, organization charts, schedules, maps, and computer networking diagrams. Once you choose to either create a new file or open an existing file (see Chapter 3 for more information on creating and opening files), Visio 2000 displays this screen. Although you can change the configuration of the screen (see Chapter 2 for more information), here you see the screen in its default mode—the way it looks when you first start using Visio 2000.

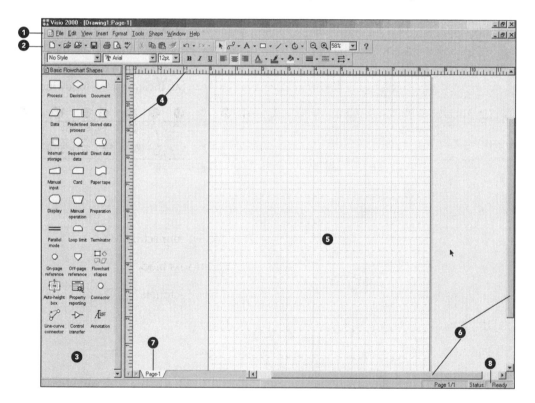

1. *Menus*—Provide all the commands available in Visio 2000.

2. *Toolbars*—Contain buttons that trigger actions; these actions duplicate the commands available in the menus. It is usually quicker to click on a button than hunt down a command in a menu. Visio 2000 supports many prebuilt toolbars, or you can build your own.

3. *Stencil*—Contains shapes that you can drag onto your diagram. You can open multiple stencils at one time. Clicking on the title bar of a stencil displays that stencil's contents.

4. *Rulers*—Provide guides for locating shapes on your diagram.

5. *Drawing area*—Build diagrams in the drawing area. It looks like a sheet of paper, giving you an idea of what your diagram will look like when you print it.

6. *Scrollbars*—Use the scrollbars to view portions of a diagram that are off screen. To scroll one line, click on an arrow at the end of a scrollbar. To scroll any amount, click and drag the bar in the middle of a scrollbar.

7. *Page tabs*—Show the pages in a Visio 2000 diagram; each page has a tab. You can jump to any page by clicking the page's tab, and you can also change the name of the page in the tab.

8. *Status line*—Provides feedback about everything from a brief description of a selected shape to hints about what to do next.

Using The Buttons In The Toolbars

Visio 2000 comes with 11 prebuilt toolbars, but only two of them—the Standard and the Format toolbars—are visible by default. Even with just these two toolbars, however, a rather daunting collection of buttons and drop-down menus are available to you, including the following:

1. Create new drawing
2. Open an existing file
3. Open a stencil
4. Save diagram
5. Print diagram
6. Print preview
7. Spellcheck
8. Cut
9. Copy
10. Paste
11. Format Painter
12. Undo

13. Redo
14. Pointer
15. Draw a connecting line
16. Create text block
17. Create rectangle
18. Draw line
19. Rotate
20. Zoom out
21. Zoom in
22. Zoom level
23. Help

Create Drawing Drop-Down Menu

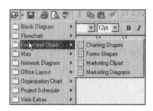

Click on the create button for a new drawing
of the same type as the one you are working
on. To create a different type of drawing, click
on the drop arrow (to the right of the button)
to drop down a menu of available drawing
types, and pick the type of drawing you want.

Stencil Drop-Down Menu

Clicking on the stencil button displays the
Open Stencil dialog box, from which you can
pick the type of stencil you want to use. If you
prefer, you can click on the drop arrow to
choose among the available stencils.

Using Format Painter

To use the Format Painter, select a shape or
block of text with the formatting you want to
duplicate in another shape or block of text.
Choose the Format Painter, and click on another shape or block of text to copy the
formatting (line color, fill, text font, and so on).

Undo And Redo Drop-Down Menus

You can actually undo or redo up to 10 actions at one time. To undo or redo multiple
actions at one time, click on the drop arrows
to the right of the undo or redo buttons to drop
down a list of all the actions you have performed. As you move the mouse pointer down
the list, all the actions from the top of the list
to the location of the mouse pointer are selected. Simply click the mouse pointer to undo
or redo all the selected actions.

Connecting Line Subtools

Two tools are hidden under the button that draws connecting lines. To access the tools, click on the drop arrow. The first of these "subtools" enables you to move the *connector points* (the point on the shape where a line anchors to the shape). The second tool is a Stamp tool. Choosing the Stamp tool enables you (after selecting a shape from a stencil) to stamp the same shape on the diagram over and over.

Line Tools: Arc, Freeform, And Pencil

Three subtools are hidden beneath the Line tool. To access these tools, click on the drop arrow. The Arc tool draws arcs of varying radii. The Freeform tool enables you to draw a line that bends any way you want. The Pencil tool is "smart." Depending on how you move your mouse, the pencil will render a straight, arc, or freeform line.

Use the line tools to create a closed shape, which you can fill with color or a pattern, by starting each new line segment at the end of the previously drawn segment. Make sure your last segment ends at the beginning point of your first segment, creating the closed shape.

Rotate Tools And Crop Tool

The first subtool under the Rotate tool enables you to move the center of rotation (the point around which the shape rotates). The other subtool is the Crop tool, which allows you to crop how much of an object imported into a Visio diagram is visible.

Modifying The Zoom Level

You can either type in the zoom level or pick the zoom level from the list of standard levels. The actual size of a diagram is 100%.

Using The Format Toolbar

Use the Format toolbar to apply styles and colors to shapes, lines, and text.

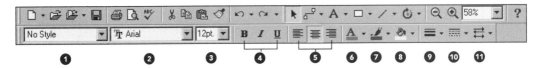

1. *Style*—Click on the drop-down menu to display and apply the available styles.

2. *Font*—Click on the drop-down menu to display and apply the available text fonts.

3. *Text size*—Click on the drop-down menu to display and apply the available sizes for the selected font. (Text is measured in points; there are 72 points in an inch.)

4. *Bold, Italic, and Underline*—Apply these font styles to selected text. If no text is selected, the next text you type will appear in the selected font style.

5. *Align left, Align center, and Align right*—Change the alignment of selected text.

6. *Text color*—Choose a text color for the selected text or, if no text is currently selected, for the next text you type. To change the color, click on the drop arrow to display a small set of colors to choose from. See the "More Text Colors" section for additional information.

7. *Line color*—Choose the line color for a selected line. To change the line color, click on the drop arrow. This displays a small set of colors to choose from. Select More Line Colors to open the Line dialog box.

8. *Fill Color*—Choose the fill color for a selected shape. To select a different fill color, click on the drop arrow. Choose More Fill Colors to open the Fill dialog box.

9. *Line weight*—Click on the button to set a selected line to the currently selected line weight. To select a different line weight, click on the drop arrow to display the list of line weights. See the "More Line Weights" section for additional information.

10. *Set line pattern*—Click on the button to set a line to the currently selected line pattern. To select a different line pattern, click on the drop arrow to the right of the button to display the list of line patterns. See the "More Line Patterns" section for additional information.

11. *Set line ends*—Click on the button to use the currently selected pair of line ends (one for the beginning and one for the end of the line). To select a different set of line ends, click on the drop arrow to display the list of available line ends. See the "More Line Ends" section for additional information.

More Text Colors

If you want to define your own color for the text color, choose More Text Colors to open the Text dialog box.

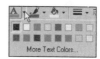

Colors In The Text Dialog Box

In the Text dialog box, you can select from the available colors by choosing from the Colors drop-down menu. Select Custom Colors from the Color drop-down menu to open a dialog box that shows all the colors your computer can produce.

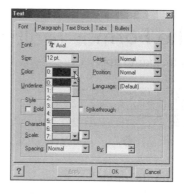

More Line Weights

If the line weights listed in the drop-down menu don't meet your needs, select additional line weights by clicking on More Line Weights. This opens the Line dialog box.

More Line Patterns

From the line patterns drop-down menu, you can select additional line patterns by choosing More Line Patterns. This opens the Line dialog box.

More Line Ends

From the line ends drop-down menu, you can select different line ends (and pick the starting and ending line ends independently) by choosing More Line Ends. This opens the Line dialog box.

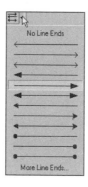

Adding Windows To The Screen

Visio 2000 has several auxiliary windows that help you keep track of information about your diagrams and the shapes in your diagrams. In addition, these windows can make it easier for you to navigate in large diagrams. This section discusses how to activate and use the Pan & Zoom, Custom Properties, and Size & Position windows.

If you find that an auxiliary window is too large or too small, simply click and drag an edge or a corner to resize the window.

The Pan & Zoom Window

To activate the Pan & Zoom window, choose Pan & Zoom from the View|Windows menu. Follow these steps to experiment with panning and zooming.

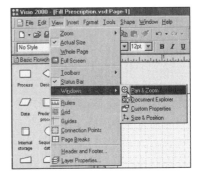

1.

Notice how the Pan & Zoom window displays a shrunken view of the entire page. It enables you to select the portion of the page you want to view, as well as the zoom level.

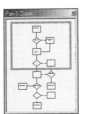

2.

By clicking and dragging the entire rectangle, you can change the portion of the page that you are viewing.

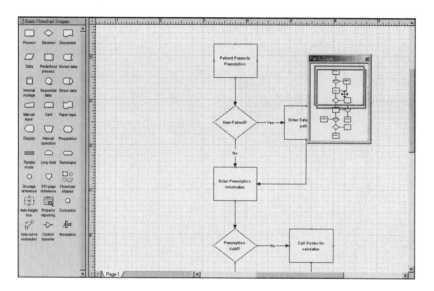

3.

By clicking and dragging an edge or corner of the rectangle, you can change how much of the page you can see—that is, the zoom level.

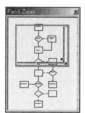

You can also click and drag a new rectangle in the Pan & Zoom window. Once you release the mouse button, the zoom level changes to match the new rectangle.

4.

You can dock the window to an edge of the screen. To do so, click on the title bar of the window and begin dragging toward an edge. When you reach an edge, the window changes into its docked version.

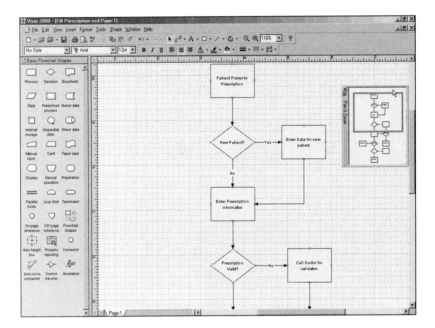

5.

Notice the pin in the upper-left corner of the docked window.

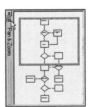

6.

If you click on the pin to deselect the button, the window collapses to display just a title bar against the edge of the screen.

To expand the docked window, simply move the mouse pointer over the collapsed title bar. To un-dock the window, drag the title bar away from the edge of the screen.

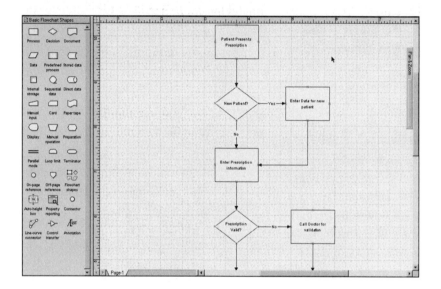

7.

You can also control the docking behavior of the window from the shortcut menu (right-click anywhere in the window to access the short-cut menu).

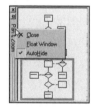

The Float Window option changes to Anchor Win-dow when the window is not docked to the edge of the screen.

The Custom Properties Window

To activate the Custom Properties window, choose Custom Properties from the View|Windows menu. The Custom Properties window displays special properties about the selected shape or line. You will learn how to define these properties in Chapter 7.

Entering Custom Properties

To enter a value for a custom property, click in the field next to the property name. Depending on the type of custom property, you can either type in a value or choose the value from a predefined list.

The Size & Position Window

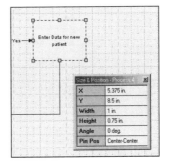

To activate the Size & Position window, choose Size & Position from the View|Windows menu. For a shape or text block, the Size & Position window displays the exact size and location of the selected shape or text block. It also shows the rotation angle and the *pin position* (the alignment point between the shape and the previously drawn shape that Visio uses to help layout the shapes).

Entering Sizes And Positions

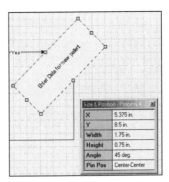

To enter a value in one of the fields in the Size & Position window, click in the field next to the property you want to change. For all fields except the Pin Pos field, type in the new value. For the Pin Pos field, choose the value you want from the drop-down menu. As you change values (for example, the Width and Angle), the shape takes on the new properties immediately.

Another Version Of The Size & Position Window

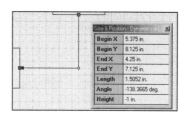

The other version of the Size & Position Window appears when you select a line or connector in the diagram. This version displays (and allows you to change) the coordinates of the starting and ending points, as well as the overall length, height, and angle of the line that would intersect both the start and endpoint.

Using the Size & Position window to modify the properties of a line or connector isn't particularly useful. If you change any of the Size & Position properties, the line will come "unstuck" from at least one of the shapes it connects.

Getting Shape Help

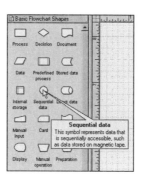

Visio 2000 comes with thousands of shapes, grouped into logical sets called *stencils*. Most of these shapes correspond to standards that are recognized by organizations throughout the world. For example, the diamond shape in a flowchart is recognized as a *decision*. However, if you aren't an expert at flowcharts (or project plans, or software design), you might not understand what a certain shape is supposed to represent.

Fortunately, Visio 2000 provides help to explain the use of each shape. Simply pause your mouse pointer over the shape, and the help information will appear.

Getting Template Help

When you create a new diagram, one of the things you can do is choose the drawing type (see Chapter 3 for more information about creating new drawings). As with shapes, the selection of drawing types can be overwhelming.

Visio 2000 provides help. When you select Choose Drawing Type from the File|New menu, Visio 2000 displays the Choose Drawing Type dialog box. Pick the category of diagram from the list on the left side of the dialog box. To get a description of each drawing type in the selected category, move your mouse pointer over the drawing types.

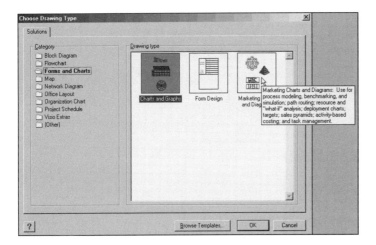

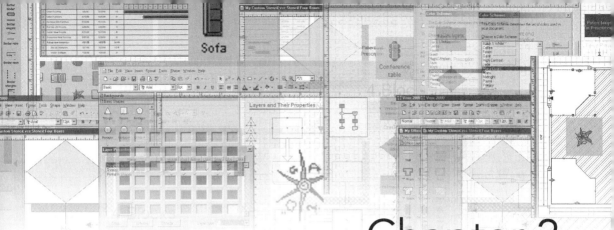

Chapter 2
Configuring Visio

- Display just the toolbars you want

- Add and remove buttons from the toolbars

- Add commands to the menus, remove commands from the menus, and rearrange the menu entries

- Set general Visio options

Customizing Toolbars, Menus, And Options

In this chapter, you will learn how to set up the Visio 2000 toolbars, menus, and general options to work the way you want. For example, you may never use the Copy and Paste buttons on the standard toolbar, preferring to use the Edit menu instead. Or, you may want to use buttons that are not present on the displayed toolbars. Visio also enables you to change the order of items on the menus (perhaps to put items you use near the top of the menu) and add or remove commands.

Configuring The Toolbars

Visio 2000 provides users with many types of toolbars—collections of buttons that trigger frequently used commands. It's easier to just click on a button than to dig through the menus for the equivalent command. However, while the default toolbar configuration is fairly useful, there are lots of ways you can change the toolbars to make them more effective for you.

Viewing Different Toolbars

Of the 11 prebuilt toolbars provided in Visio 2000, only two are visible by default—the Standard and Format toolbars.

To view a complete list of the available toolbars, right-click on any toolbar to display the shortcut menu.

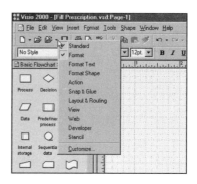

Showing And Hiding Toolbars

The toolbars with a checkmark next to their name are currently visible. To make another toolbar visible, simply click next to the toolbar name to turn the toolbar on. For example, if you click next to the Snap & Glue toolbar name, the Snap & Glue toolbar becomes visible. (In the illustration, it is at the end of the bottom row of toolbar buttons.)

Alternatively, to hide a visible toolbar, click next to a toolbar name to remove the checkmark.

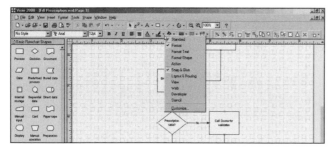

Selecting View|Toolbars

You can also perform all of these actions by selecting View|Toolbars.

Customize Dialog Box

To further customize the toolbars, choose Customize from the toolbar shortcut menu or the View|Toolbars menu. This displays the Customize dialog box. From this dialog box, you can also turn toolbars off and on by selecting the checkboxes alongside each toolbar name.

If you clear the Menu Bar entry, you can hide the menus at the top of the screen.

Rearranging Buttons

Once the Customize dialog box is open, you can start changing the toolbars. First, you can rearrange the order of the buttons by dragging a button to a new location. For example, click on the Printer button and drag it. As you move the button, a black I-beam cursor displays where the button will be located when you release the mouse button.

Deleting Buttons

You can delete a button from the toolbar by dragging it completely off the toolbar. The "x" mouse cursor shape indicates that when you release the left mouse button, the selected button (in this case, the Print button) will be deleted from the toolbar.

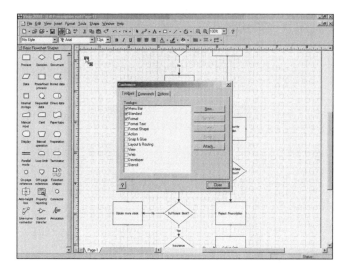

Using Button Shortcuts

Right-click on a button to access its shortcut menu. From the shortcut menu, you can reset the button to its factory default, delete the button, change its name (enter a new name in the Name field), display the button with a graphic, text, or both, and add a faint divider to the left of the button by selecting the Begin A Group option.

Changing Button Images

You can also change the button image by choosing a new image from the images presented when you click on the Change Button Image option on the shortcut menu.

If you make a total mess out of a prebuilt toolbar, you can undo all of your changes and put the toolbar back the way it was when you installed Visio 2000. To do so, click on the name of the toolbar in the Toolbars list of the Customize dialog box, and then click on the Reset button. You cannot Reset your custom toolbars.

Creating New Toolbars

Beyond rearranging, deleting, and changing the buttons on toolbars, you can start from scratch and create a new toolbar.

1.

To create a new toolbar from the Customize dialog box, click on the New button. Name your new toolbar by typing the name into the Toolbar Name field.

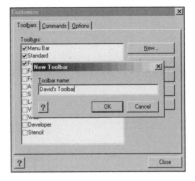

2.

Click on OK. This creates a new, empty toolbar and adds the toolbar to the list of available toolbars in the Customize dialog box.

3.

To populate the new toolbar, switch to the Commands tab of the Customize dialog box.

4.

Choose a category from the list on the left side of the dialog box, then choose a command from the Commands list on the right side. Drag the command to the new toolbar to add buttons to it.

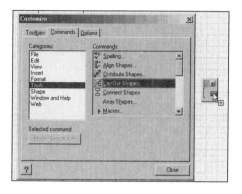

You can drag commands to existing toolbars (such as those at the top of the screen) to add buttons to those toolbars as well.

5.

Continue adding buttons until you have the new toolbar looking just the way you want.

You can change the name of any of your custom toolbars. From the Toolbars tab of the Customize dialog box, click on the custom toolbar, and then click the Rename button. Enter a new name and click on OK. You cannot rename prebuilt toolbars.

Resizing A Floating Toolbar

Toolbars can either "float" on the screen like a regular window or "dock" to the edge of the screen. If the toolbar is floating, you can resize it by dragging a corner or an edge. As you change the size, the buttons rearrange automatically to fit the new size.

Docking A Toolbar

To dock a floating toolbar to the edge of the screen, drag the toolbar to the edge to which you want to dock it. For example, I dragged the new toolbar to the bottom edge of the diagram to dock it there.

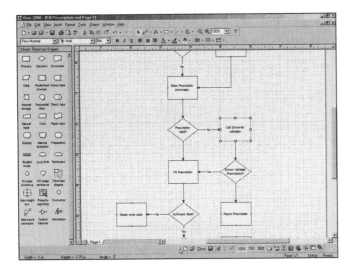

Docking To Other Toolbars

You can also drag a docked toolbar back onto the screen, converting it to a window. Or, you can drag it alongside another toolbar, where it can coexist with that toolbar as long as there is room. For example, I dragged the new toolbar into the toolbar area at the top of the screen, where it takes up residence alongside the existing Format toolbar.

Configuring The Commands And Menus

Unlike many other applications, Visio 2000's menus are just as configurable as the toolbars. You can rearrange the menus, add and remove commands, and even build completely custom menus.

As with configuring toolbars, you must open the Customize dialog box by either choosing Customize from the toolbar shortcut menu or selecting View|Toolbars|Customize from the menus.

Rearranging Menus

You can change the order of the entries on the top-level menu (File, Edit, View, and so on). Simply click and drag the item to a new location. As with toolbar buttons, a dark I-beam cursor appears to show you where the menu will be located when you release the mouse button. In the example, I dragged the Format menu to the right of the Tools menu.

Deleting Menus

To remove a top-level menu item entirely, click on it and drag it away from the menu bar.

Reordering Menu Items

Within a given menu, you can rearrange the order of the items. To do so, click on an item and drag it to its new location on the menu. For example, you could relocate the Microsoft Graph entry to the top of the Insert menu if you use graphs frequently.

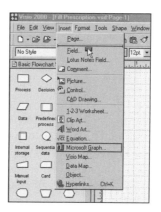

Swapping Items Between Menus

You can also move items from one menu to another. Click on the menu to drop it down, and then click on the item you want to move. Drag it to the destination menu, and pause until the menu drops down. Then, drag the menu item to its new location on the new menu. For example, I have moved the Color Palette item from the Tools menu to the Format menu.

Removing Menu Options

To remove an item from a menu altogether, click on the menu to drop it down, click on the item, and drag it off the menu. For example, I have deleted the Shadow item from the Format menu.

Adding Items To Menus

Similar to relocating items from one menu to another, you can add items to a menu by dragging commands from the Commands tab of the Customize dialog box. For example, to add the Connect Shapes command to the Edit menu, choose Tools in the Categories list. Click on the Connect Shapes command in the Commands list, and drag it to the Edit menu. Pause while the menu drops down, and drag the command to its new location on the Edit menu.

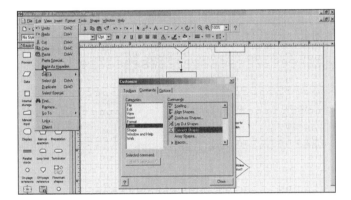

Working With Shortcut Menus

Each item on a menu has a shortcut menu of its own. You can reset or delete the item, change its name, change or reset the image, change the display style, and add a separator just above the item by selecting Begin A Group.

Setting The General Options

The Options tab of the Customize dialog box provides additional configuration options for toolbars and menus.

Setting Icon Size

You can set the size of the icons, show the ScreenTips when you hold the mouse cursor over a button, and show the shortcut keys in the ScreenTips. If you check Large Icons, the toolbar icons are considerably enlarged (as shown in the screenshot) making them easier to see, but they take up a lot more room on the screen.

Showing ScreenTips

The Show ScreenTips On Toolbars option provides small pop-up flags that tell you the name of the toolbar button.

Showing Shortcut Keys

The Show Shortcut Keys In ScreenTips option displays the keyboard shortcut (if there is one) for the toolbar button in the ScreenTip for that button.

Using Animations

You can also use animations when the menus drop down—a useless but fun enhancement. When the Menu Animations is set to None, a drop-down menu simply appears when you click on it. If you select one of the animations, a drop-down menu slides or unfolds onto the screen. To choose an animation, select it from the Menu Animations drop-down list.

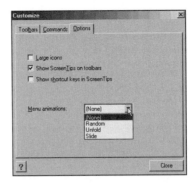

Setting The Main Options

You can configure Visio to change many of its properties. You'll probably never need to change many of these options, but you're likely to visit some of them from time to time. These include setting the number of levels of undo, page colors, spellcheck options, and file paths. To specify your choices, select Tools|Options to open the Options dialog box.

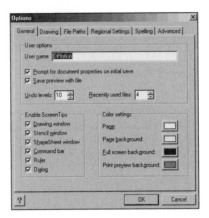

Setting The General Options

From the General tab of the Options dialog box, you can set the user name and whether to display the document properties dialog box the first time you save the file or to save a preview with the file. If you save a preview of the file, the preview appears when you click on the file from the Open dialog box.

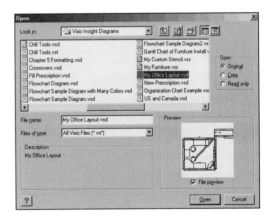

Undo Levels And Recently Used Files

You can also set the number of levels of Undo (up to a maximum of 99) by either entering a number into the Undo Levels field or by using the spinner to increase or decrease the number. The Recently Used Files field works similarly—the specified number of recently used files (up to a maximum of nine) appears in the Files menu.

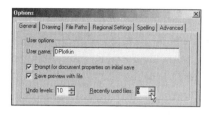

Recently Used Files List

The actual file names of the recently used files appear at the end of the File menu.

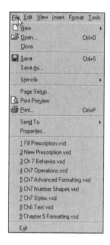

Enable ScreenTips

By placing a checkmark alongside the choices in the Enable ScreenTips section, you can specify which items you want the ScreenTips to appear with when you hold the mouse over the item.

Color Settings

The Color Settings section enables you to set the color of a page, page background, full screen background, and print preview background. To set a color, click on the colored button to the right of the item you want to change. This opens the Edit Color dialog box.

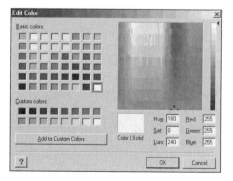

From the Edit Color dialog box, you can choose one of the Basic Colors, one of the Custom Colors, any color from the large color block, or enter values for Hue/Sat/Lum or Red/Green/Blue to specify a color. If you want to save the color to the custom color area, simply click the Add To Custom Colors button.

Setting The File Paths

Visio needs to know where to look for items such as Templates, Stencils, Help files, and any Add-ons. In addition, it needs to know what default path to use to save your own files. You can set all these paths from the File Paths tab of the Options dialog box.

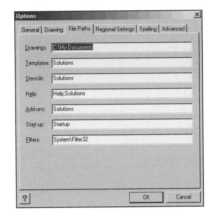

Setting The Spell Checker Options

Visio also includes a spell checker you can use to avoid spelling errors in your text blocks and the text you embed in shapes. To set the spellcheck options, select Tools|Options and click on the Spelling tab.

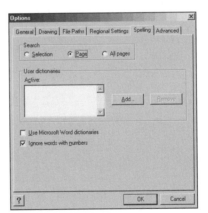

If you have Microsoft Office and have installed the Word spell checker, you can have Visio use that instead of its own spell checker. Just select the Use Microsoft Word Dictionaries checkbox.

Add User Dictionary

If you want to save your own words to the spell checker, you'll have to add at least one User Dictionary. To do so, click on the Add button to open the Add User Dictionary dialog box. Create a new dictionary or choose an existing dictionary from this dialog box.

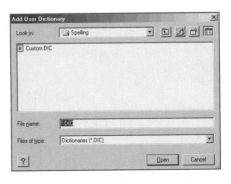

Chapter 3
Creating Your First
Visio Diagram

- Learn to create a new diagram

- Open and close stencils to gain
  access to collections of shapes

- Add, delete, and move shapes on
  a diagram

- Connect shapes with lines

- Add text to a diagram

Creating A New Diagram

You are through with the preliminaries, and it's time to start creating diagrams in Visio. In this chapter you will learn how to create a new diagram in a variety of ways and set the properties of the output and the file itself. In addition, you'll learn how to open and close stencils and work with multiple stencils so you use the shapes on multiple stencils to build a diagram. To build a diagram, you need to drag shapes onto the drawing area, connect those shapes, and add text to the diagram—either within a shape or as an independent text block. By the time you finish this chapter, you will understand how to perform all these tasks.

The first step in building your own Visio drawing is to create a new diagram. Visio actually provides two ways to do this. You can create a new drawing from a template (the most common way) or from a blank diagram.

Creating A New Diagram From A Template

To create a new diagram from a template, select File|New to view the list of drawing categories. Move the mouse over one of the categories and choose the type of drawing you want from the list that appears on the menu.

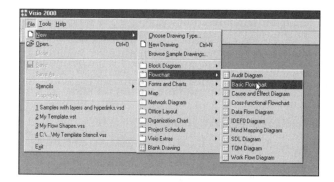

Open A New Diagram

The new diagram opens with the appropriate stencil(s) and a blank drawing area.

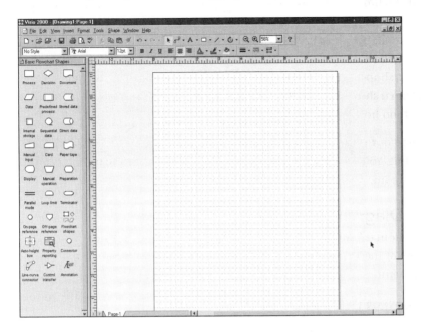

Choose Drawing Type Dialog Box

Another way to create a new diagram from a template is to select Choose Drawing Type from the File|New menu. This action opens the Choose Drawing Type dialog box.

Select a category from the Category list. To select one of the diagram types in a category, double-click on it or highlight it and click on OK.

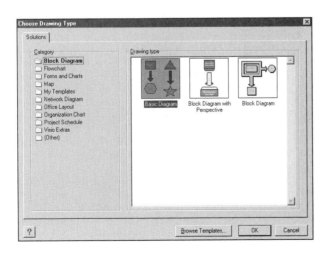

Sample Drawings

Visio 2000 also comes with a collection of sample diagrams that you can use as a starting point for your own work. To use one of these drawings, select File|New|Browse Sample Drawings to view the Browse Sample Drawings dialog box.

Double-click on one of the sample folders to open it and choose a sample diagram.

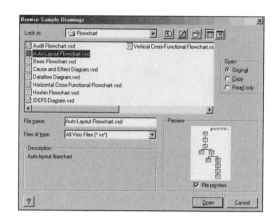

To avoid changing the sample diagram, make sure you choose the Copy radio button in the Open section of the dialog box. This allows you to change and save a copy without affecting the original.

Starter Diagrams

Many of the templates provide a starter diagram to get you going. This can be very helpful, especially if you are not an expert with the methodology that the diagram supports. For example, if you select Cause And Effect Diagram from the Flowchart category, Visio provides this diagram (also known as a "fishbone" diagram) to get you going.

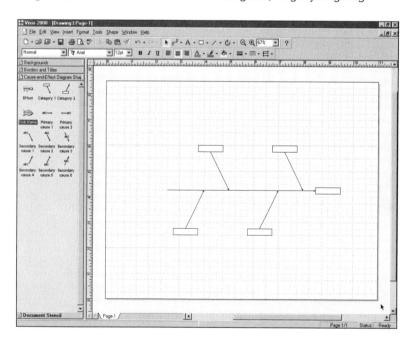

Creating A New Diagram From A Blank Diagram

If you want to build your own diagram from scratch and specify the use of stencils, you can create a blank drawing with no default stencil by selecting File|New|New Drawing.

Stencils will be covered in the "Working With Stencils" section later in this chapter.

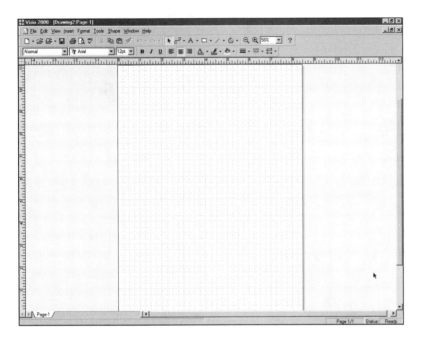

Setting File Properties

Once you've created a diagram, you can set its File properties by selecting File|Properties to open the Properties dialog box. Click on the Summary tab if it isn't already visible. By adding information such as the Title, Subject, Author, Category, Keywords, and Description, you should be able to recall the reason you created this diagram and what it is used for at a later date.

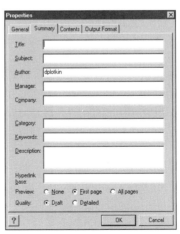

Setting The Output Format

Visio can customize the diagram output depending on its final destination. To set the final destination, choose the Output Format tab from the Properties dialog box. Click on the format of the final output: Printing, Microsoft PowerPoint Slide Show, or HTML Or GIF Output (for the Internet).

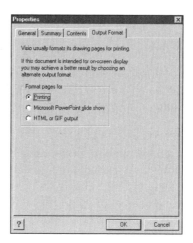

Adding Drawing Tools To The Screen

Visio provides a number of auxiliary drawing tools that will help you align items and position them on the screen. To turn these tools on and off, select the View menu. Grouped near the bottom of the menu are the entries Rulers, Grid, Guides, Connection Points, and Page Breaks. These menu items are toggles; clicking on the item turns it on and off. When the image next to the menu item is depressed, the feature is enabled and visible.

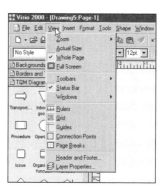

Using The Rulers

When you turn the rulers on, a pair of rulers border the screen—one at the top of the screen and one at the left edge. These rulers help measure the distance from the edges of the page. The ruler at the top measures the distance from the left edge of the page; the ruler at the left side measures the distance from the *bottom* edge of the page.

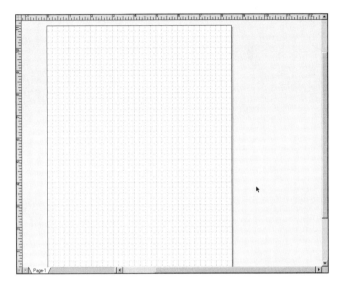

Relocate The Vertical Ruler Zero Point

You can reset the zero point for each of the rulers. To reset the zero point of the vertical ruler (located at the left edge of the screen), hold down the Ctrl key and drag a line from the ruler at the top of the screen. Release the mouse button, and the zero point of the vertical ruler is relocated to coincide with the line you dragged.

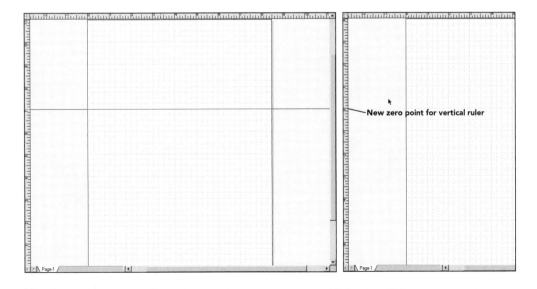

New zero point for vertical ruler

Relocate The Horizontal Ruler Zero Point

To reset the zero point of the horizontal ruler (located at the top of the screen), hold down the Ctrl key and drag a line from the ruler at the left edge of the screen. The zero point for the horizontal ruler is relocated to coincide with the line you dragged.

To reset a ruler's zero point back to the default, double-click on the ruler. To reset both rulers' zero points at the same time, double-click in the rectangle between the rulers in the upper-left corner of the drawing area.

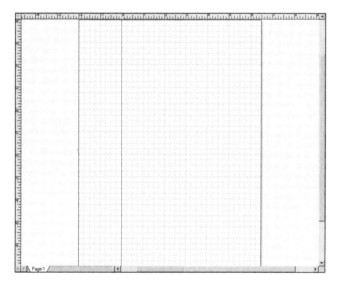

Using The Grid

By default, Visio 2000 provides a grid of lines in the background to help you align the objects you place on the diagram (you can see the grid in the previous graphic). If you find the grid distracting, you can turn it off, which will leave you with a nice, clean "sheet of paper."

Using The Guides

Although the grids and rulers are helpful in aligning objects, you can establish either horizontal or vertical guides on the screen and align objects to those guides. To use the guides, make sure that the Guides option is selected in the View menu.

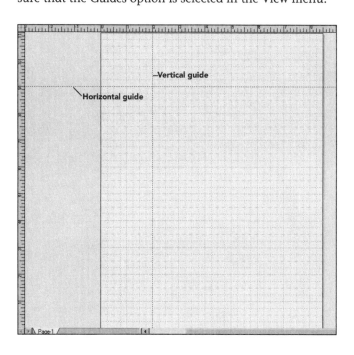

To delete a guide, click on it and press the Delete
key or select Cut from the guide's shortcut menu.

Establishing A Vertical Guide

To establish a vertical guide, move the mouse pointer to the vertical ruler until it becomes a double-headed arrow; then drag the guide onto the page.

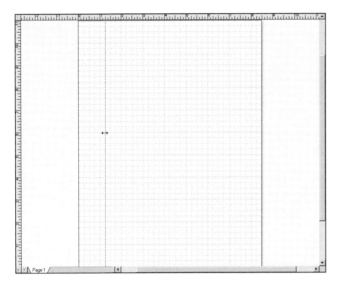

To establish a horizontal guide, move the mouse pointer to the horizontal ruler until it becomes a double-headed arrow; then drag the guide onto the page.

Relocating Guides

Once the guide is on the page, you can relocate it by clicking and dragging it to a new location.

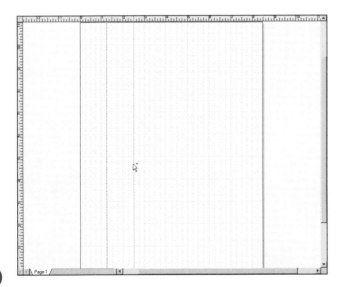

Creating A Guide Point

In addition to guide lines, you can create a guide "point" as well. To do so, click in the rectangle at the upper-left corner of the drawing area and drag it onto the diagram. A pair of lines appear; the intersection of those lines show where the guide point will be located.

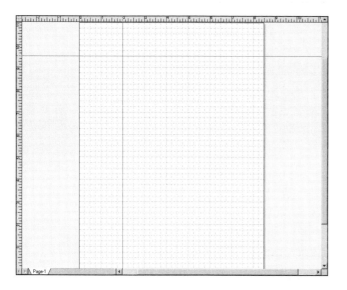

Placing A Guide Point

When you release the mouse button, Visio 2000 places a guide point on the page.

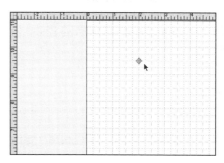

Showing Connection Points

Connection points are special points, usually located on the perimeter of a shape to which connecting lines will "anchor" themselves. If you attach a line to a shape at a connecting point, and then move the shape, the line will remain attached—rerouting itself as necessary. Connection points are usually displayed as small "x" symbols on the shape.

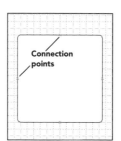

Connection points

Hiding Connection Points

If you turn off the Connection Points on the View menu, the connection points will no longer be visible.

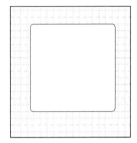

Showing Page Breaks

Page Breaks separate a Visio 2000 diagram into printable pages. The nonprintable areas (for example, the quarter-inch area around the edges that a laser printer cannot print on) are shaded in gray, and a line denotes the edges of the physical printed page.

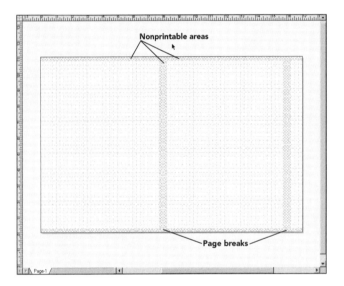

Saving A File

Once you've completed some work on a diagram, you'll want to save that work as a file to your hard drive. The first time you save a file you can select either File|Save or File|Save As. Either way, Visio 2000 opens the Save As dialog box so you can name the file and choose its location.

Name The File

Type the name of the file into the File Name field and choose whether to save the Workspace or not. If you save the Workspace, the diagram and its stencils open the next time you open the file; otherwise, only the diagram opens.

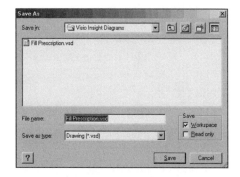

Choose The File Location

You can navigate through the structure of your hard drive to specify where to save the file by clicking on the Save In drop-down list.

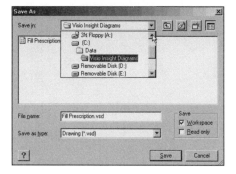

Create A New Folder

If you need to create a new folder for the diagram, click on the Create New Folder button. This creates a new folder (called New Folder) in the current directory, which you can rename at any time.

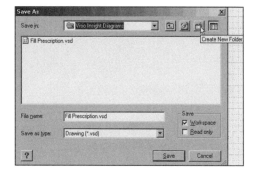

Once you have saved a file for the first time, clicking File|Save just resaves the file by the same name, overwriting the previous version. If you want to preserve the previous version, select File|Save As, and follow the steps discussed earlier.

Working With Stencils

Stencils are groups of shapes from which you can choose to drag shapes onto a drawing. They appear by default at the left edge of a diagram when you first create the drawing. Depending on the type of diagram you create, one or more stencils are initially available. You can close a stencil you are not going to use or open another stencil that contains shapes you need. This section teaches you how to open and close stencils and move them around the screen to make them easier to use.

Opening Stencils

To open a new stencil, select File|Stencils to display the list of stencil categories. Move the mouse over a category to display the list of stencils in that category and click on the stencil you want to add to the diagram.

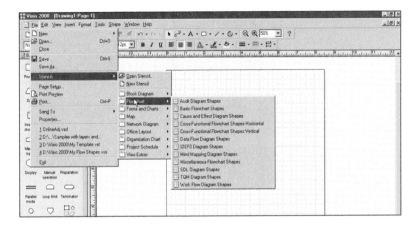

Open Stencil Dialog Box

You can also choose a stencil by selecting File|Stencils|Open Stencil to display the Open Stencil dialog box.

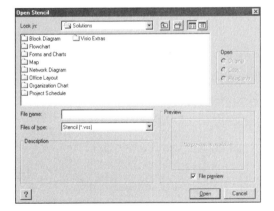

Stencil Description Field

Double-click on one of the stencil category folders and click on the stencil you want. The Description field defines what the stencil is used for.

Click on the Open button to open the stencil. Normally, you'll want to open the stencil as read only (select the Read Only radio button). However, if you want to modify the stencil it-self (as described in Chapter 8), open the stencil as Original.

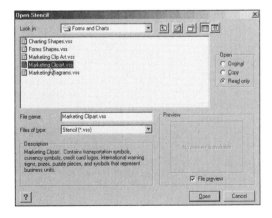

Changing Stencil Properties

Stencils have a shortcut menu, which you can access by either right-clicking on the stencil's title bar or left-clicking on the left corner of the stencil's title bar. From this menu, you can choose how to display the stencil shapes (icons and names, icons only, or names only), close the stencil, or save the stencil by a different name.

Changing The Stencil Position

Similar to the auxiliary property windows, stencils can be either docked to the edge of the screen (the default is the left edge) or positioned as a free-floating window. To change the position of a stencil, choose Position from the shortcut menu.

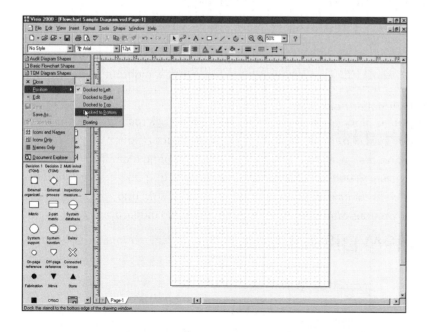

Dock A Stencil

Select the new position from the Position menu (for example, Docked To Bottom) and the stencil will relocate to match the selected position.

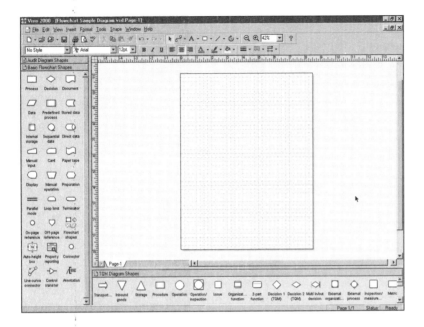

Drag A Stencil

You can also relocate the stencil by dragging it to a new position. To do so, click on the stencil title bar and drag the stencil to its destination. If the destination is close to an edge of the screen, the stencil will dock to that edge; otherwise, the stencil floats as a separate window that you can resize and move.

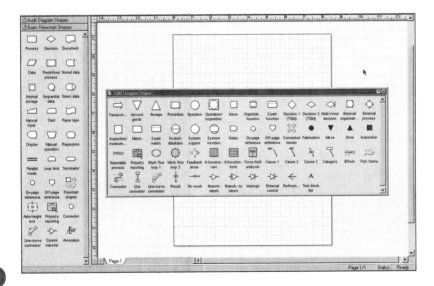

Working With Multiple Stencils

If you dock multiple stencils to the same edge of the screen (for example, the default left edge), the contents of only one stencil is visible at a time. The other stencils display only their title bars.

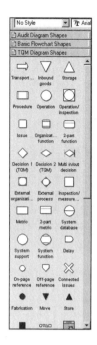

Viewing Another Stencil

To view the contents of another stencil, click the title bar of that stencil. Any stencils that are on top of the selected stencil move out of the way. For example, if three stencils are docked to the left edge of the screen and you click on the second stencil's title bar (Basic Flowchart Shapes in the example), the second stencil becomes visible and the title bar of the top (first) stencil (TQM Diagram Shapes in the example) moves to the bottom of the screen.

Working With Shapes And Lines

In this section, you actually begin to build Visio 2000 diagrams. Because a Visio drawing consists primarily of shapes connected by lines, this section will focus on working with shapes and lines.

Adding Shapes By Dragging

The first step in building a diagram is to add shapes to the drawing.

1.

The most common way to add a shape to the diagram is to drag the shape you want from the stencil onto the drawing area.

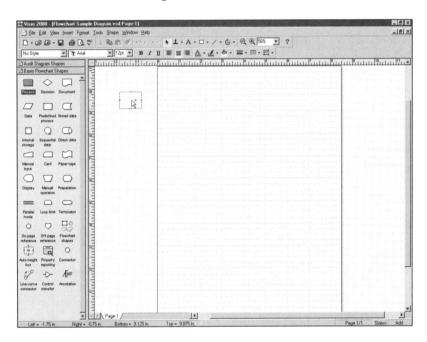

2.

Once the shape is positioned properly, simply release the left mouse button to place the shape on the page.

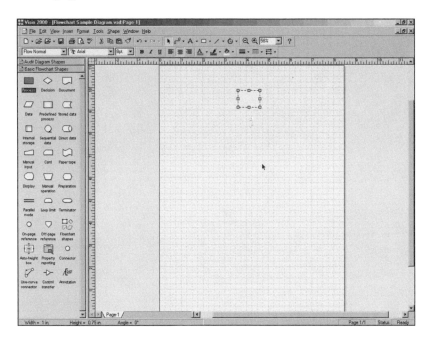

3.

If you are going to connect a new shape to the currently selected shape (via a line), there is an easy way to add both the new shape and the connector to the diagram. To perform this function, choose the Connector tool from the toolbar.

4.

Select a shape and drag the shape onto the
diagram. Visio 2000 automatically connects
the new shape to the previously selected shape.

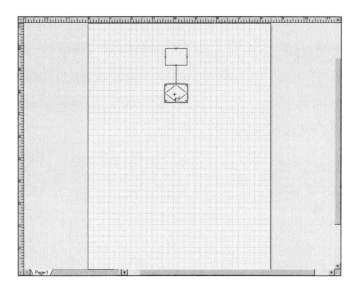

Adding Shapes With The Stamp Tool

If you are going to be adding a few copies of a particular shape, consider using the Stamp tool.

1.

To choose the Stamp tool, click on the drop
arrow alongside the Connector tool on the
toolbar. Choose the Stamp tool from the resulting drop-down list.

2.

Click on the shape in the stencil that you want
to use as a stamp. This "picks up" the shape.
Then move the Stamp onto the drawing and
begin clicking. Each click draws another copy
of the selected shape.

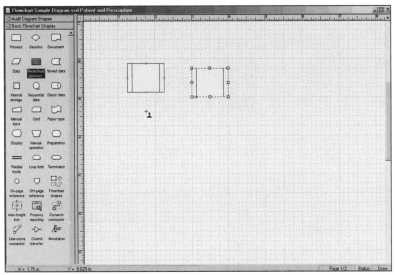

Connecting Shapes With The Connector Tool

If you have placed some shapes on the drawing and want to connect them, you can use either
the Connector tool from the toolbar or one of the connector shapes in the stencil.

1.

To connect two shapes using the Connector tool,
choose the Connector tool from the toolbar.
Place the mouse near one of the connection
points on the first shape (designated by the
small "x" symbols on the shape). Visio lets you
know when you're on a connection point.

2.

Click and drag the connector to the connection point on another shape.

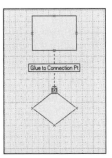

3.

Release the mouse button to finish drawing the connector.

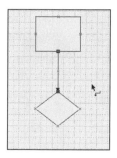

Connecting Shapes With Stencil Connectors

You can also connect shapes using the connectors that are present in most stencils. This graphic shows that two connector shapes are included with the Audit Diagram Shapes stencil.

1.

To link two shapes using a connector shape, click and drag the connector shape onto the drawing area, making sure that one end of the connector shape touches a connection point on a shape.

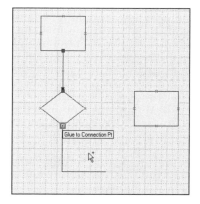

2.

Release the mouse button, and the connector shape is drawn with one end anchored to the shape you selected.

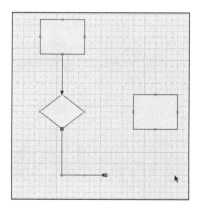

3.

Now drag the other (unanchored) end of the connector shape to the connection point on another shape.

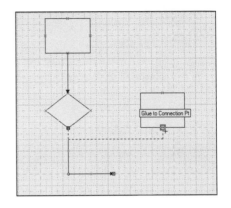

4.

The line automatically finds the best route between the two shapes. Release the mouse button to draw the connector shape.

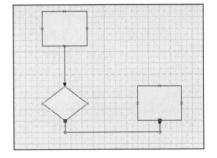

Moving Shapes

You may find that you need to move shapes around on a drawing.

1.

To move a shape, select the Pointer tool, click on the shape, and drag it to its new location.

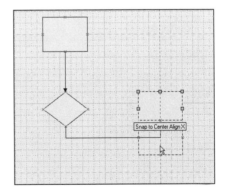

2.

Any lines connected to the shape's connection points are automatically rerouted and remain connected to the shape.

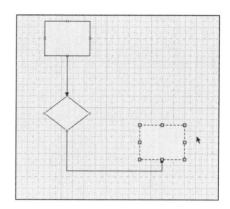

3.

Of course, it may make sense to change the connection point for a connector. To do so, click on the connector to select it (the connection points display red "+" symbols). Then click and drag one of the ends to a different connection point.

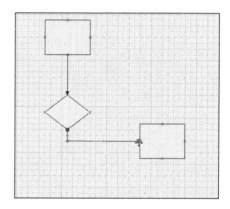

Rerouting Connection Lines

Once you've connected some shapes with connectors, you can reroute those lines either manually or with some help from Visio 2000. A connector has two distinct characteristics: *handles* and *vertexes*. A handle is denoted by a green "x"; a vertex is present on the connector anywhere it changes direction and is denoted by a green diamond. The area between two vertexes, between a vertex and a handle, or between a vertex and a connection to a shape is known as a *segment*.

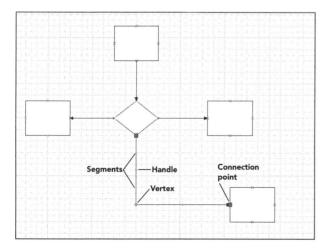

Understanding Vertexes And Handles

It is important to understand the difference between handles and vertexes because each behaves differently when you click and drag it.

1.

Try clicking and dragging a vertex.

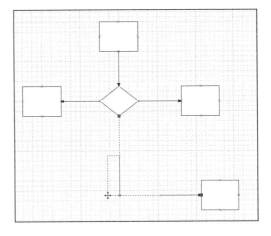

2.

Visio 2000 adds additional segments (each with its own handle) to ensure that the connection point remains connected to the shape.

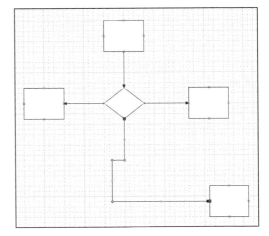

3.

Normally, when you click and drag a vertex, Visio 2000 creates new segments in such a way that the segments are all either horizontal or vertical (as illustrated in the previous graphic). However, if you want a single segment to join the two endpoints, hold down the Ctrl key while dragging the vertex.

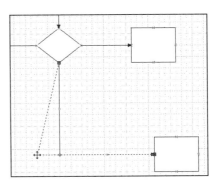

4.

Dragging a handle leads to a slightly different result.

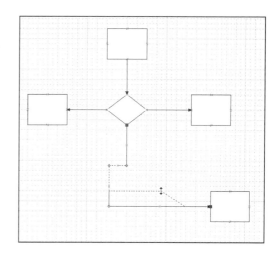

5.

If you simply drag the handle, the handle's
segment moves, along with the vertexes that
mark the endpoints of the segment. However,
if you hold down the Ctrl key while dragging
the handle, the handle becomes the vertex of
a new line segment, and Visio 2000 adds segments to ensure that the connection points
remain connected. It may also relocate some
existing vertexes.

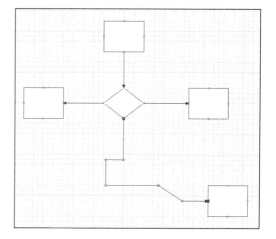

Using Connector Shortcuts

A connector's shortcut menu provides some
options for rerouting the connectors with Visio
2000's help.

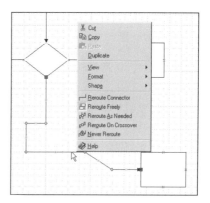

---

*To access the shortcut menu, right-click on the con-
nector. Right-clicking is the standard technique for
accessing shortcut menus.*

Using Visio's Rerouting

To have Visio 2000 reroute a connector, choose Reroute Connector from the connector's shortcut menu.

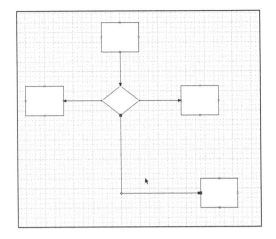

More Visio Rerouting

Unless you have the Never Reroute option selected in the shortcut menu, Visio 2000 will also reroute a connector for you if you either drop a new shape on the connector or move an existing shape on top of the connector.

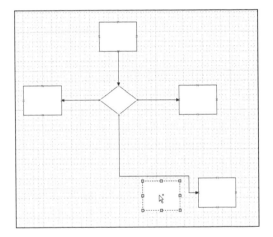

Adding Text To A Drawing

The amount of information you can communicate using a drawing that contains just lines and shapes is significantly limited. You need to add text to a diagram to provide explanations for the purpose of the shapes and lines, as well as general explanations about the drawing itself. The following sections show you how to add text to shapes and lines. In addition, you'll find out how to add independent text blocks to the drawing. Chapter 6 details how to format your text.

Adding Text To A Shape

This section shows you how to add text to shapes. Ways to modify text also are covered.

1.

To add text to a shape, click on the shape to select it and begin typing. As soon as you begin to type, the text appears in the shape.

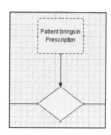

2.

Once you add text to all the shapes, you can see how much more informative the drawing is.

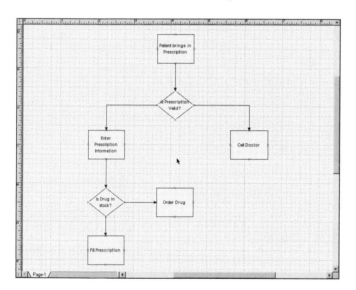

3.

There are two ways to edit the text in a shape. If you haven't modified the shape's behavior, you can double-click on the shape, select the text you want to change, and type the new text.

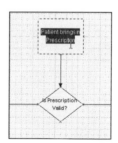

To replace all the text in a shape, click on the shape and begin typing. The new text you type completely replaces the existing text.

4.

Another way to edit the text in a shape is to
select the Text tool from the toolbar. When the
mouse is over existing text in a shape, the
mouse pointer turns into the I-beam text edit
cursor. Select the text you want to change and
type the new text.

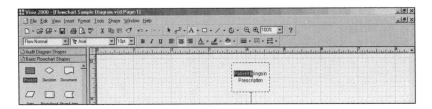

Adding Text To Connectors

This section shows you how to add text to lines and then edit the text, if needed.

1.

You can add text to connectors the same way
you do with shapes; just click on the line and
begin typing.

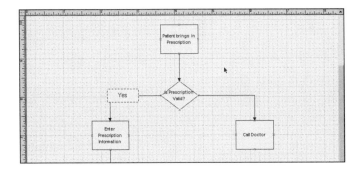

2.

Once again, a fully labeled diagram is much
more informative.

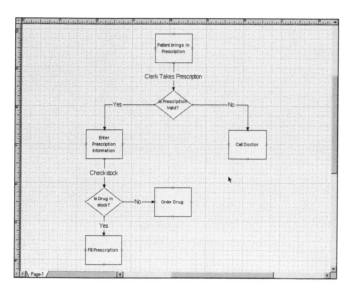

3.

Similar to a shape, you can edit the text in a
connector by double-clicking on it (if you
haven't modified the default behavior) or by
choosing the Text tool from the toolbar and
selecting the text you want to change.

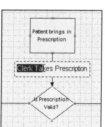

Adding Text Blocks

You can add blocks of text that label or explain various portions of your diagram.

1.

To add a text block, select the Text tool from the toolbar. Drag a rectangular area onto the drawing to define the boundaries of the text block.

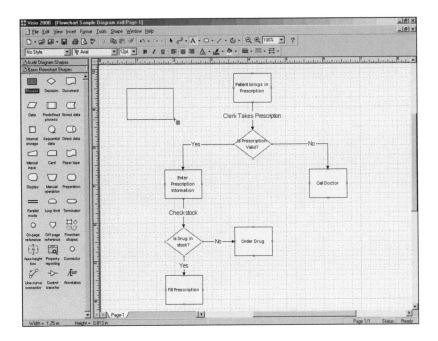

2.

Release the mouse pointer to create the text block; it is now ready for typing.

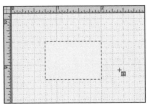

3.

Type in the text for the text block.

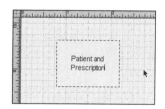

4.

You can also edit the text in a text block by double-clicking on it (if you haven't modified the default behavior) or by choosing the Text tool from the toolbar and selecting the text you want to change.

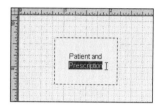

Chapter 4
Changing Page And
Drawing Properties

- Learn to add pages to a drawing and set the page properties

- Adjust the page-oriented drawing tools, such as snap and glue

- Choose color schemes and palettes

- Set up backgrounds, headers, and footers

- Print your drawing

Adjusting The Page Properties

Visio 2000 includes powerful tools that help you lay out your drawing. These include the rulers, snap and glue, and the grid. In this section, you learn to set the properties for these tools, as well as the properties of each drawing page. You will also learn to add pages and print your diagram.

Setting The Drawing Size And Orientation

To set the drawing size and orientation, select File|Page Setup and click on the Page Size tab.

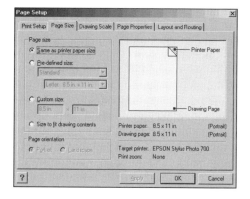

The default setting for the page size corresponds to the page size for your printer.

Setting A Pre-Defined Page Size

To change the page size, click on the Pre-Defined Size radio button. From the top drop-down menu, choose any of the standard paper types; from the lower drop-down menu, choose paper sizes in the selected category. If the size you choose doesn't match the printer paper size, Visio displays this fact in the dialog box.

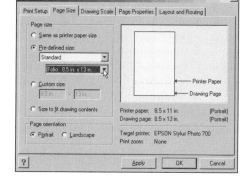

Setting A Custom Page Size

You can enter a custom size if none of the standard sizes match your paper. To do so, click on the Custom Size radio button and enter the drawing size in the Custom Size text fields.

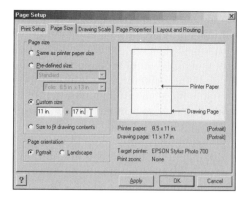

Fitting Page Size To Drawing Contents

To dynamically size the page to the drawing contents, choose the Size To Fit Drawing Contents radio button.

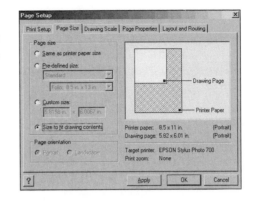

Setting The Page Orientation

You can set the page orientation for both pre-defined and custom sizes by clicking on either the Portrait or the Landscape radio buttons in the Page Orientation section of the dialog box. The Portrait choice is longer vertically, and the Landscape choice is longer horizontally (as shown here).

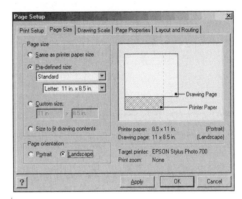

Choosing A Drawing Scale

By default, the rulers display one inch for every inch of the paper, known as 1:1. However, you might want the rulers to display an architectural scale of $^1/_4$"=1'0" for a large object (such as a building). To set the drawing scale, choose the Drawing Scale tab of the Page Setup dialog box.

Choosing A Pre-Defined Scale

Pre-defined scales are drawing scales commonly used by professionals, such as architects or mechanical engineers. Visio provides a set of pre-defined scales for you to use.

1.

To choose a standard pre-defined scale, choose the Pre-Defined Scale radio button.

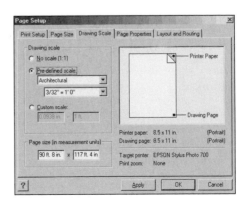

2.

Choose one of the types of scales in the first drop-down menu. The most common type of scale is architectural, used for things such as office layouts, street plans, and so on.

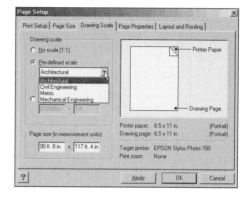

3.

Choose the exact scale you want to use from the second drop-down menu. Notice that Visio 2000 shows you how much (in the selected scale) will fit on the page in the Page Size section of the dialog box (lower-left corner).

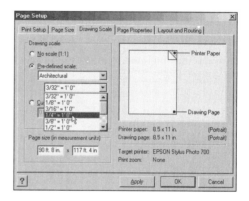

Choosing A Custom Scale

If none of the pre-defined scales meet your needs, you can set up a custom scale by clicking on the Custom Scale radio button. Then, type the two quantities that define the scale in the Custom Scale fields.

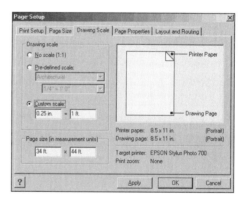

Setting The Page Properties

You can set the page name, measurement units, shape shadow offset, and background (covered in more detail later in this chapter) from the Page Properties tab of the Page Setup dialog box.

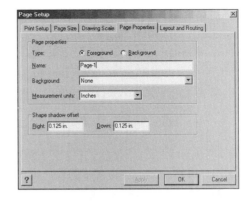

Naming A Page

To change the page name (which also appears on the page tab), type a new name into the Name field.

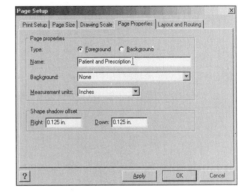

Setting Measurement Units

Set the measurement units displayed in the rulers from the Measurement Units drop-down menu.

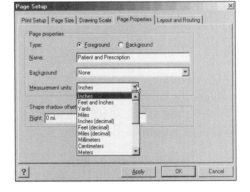

The Shape Shadow Offset is the distance that the shadow for a shape is offset from the shape itself. To change this quantity, type the new offsets into the Shape Shadow Offset section. Larger numbers display more of the shadow.

Setting Layout And Routing Properties

The properties you set in the Layout And Routing tab of the Page Setup dialog box affect how the connectors are drawn when you connect shapes.

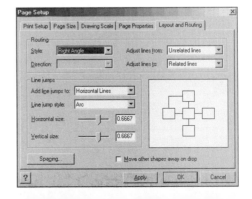

Routing Section

The information in the routing section controls how connector lines are drawn. The
default value of Right Angle in the Style drop-
down menu always routes lines with
right-angle bends in them.

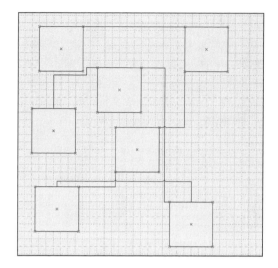

Changing The Style Default

You can choose a different value from the Style
drop-down menu and see the change in the
preview area.

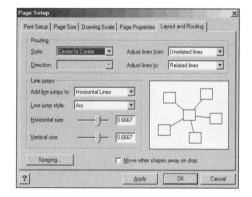

Direction Option

Some Style options (such as the Flowchart option) have a Direction option you can choose
from the Direction drop-down menu.

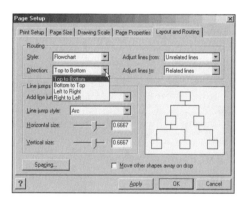

Line Jumps

It can be difficult to distinguish between connector lines when they cross each other. To help
with this situation, you can add "line jumps"
to lines when they cross. Choose which type of
lines to add jumps to from the Add Line Jumps
To drop-down menu.

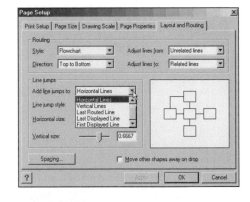

Setting Line Jump Styles

You can set the style of the line jump from the
Line Jump Style drop-down menu.

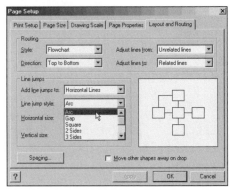

Sizing Line Jumps

Finally, you can set the horizontal and vertical
size of the line jumps using the sliders at the
bottom of the dialog box. Larger jumps are
easier to see, but they may be more unwieldy.

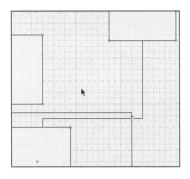

Layout And Routing Spacing

Visio 2000 enables you to set the spacing between shapes, average shape size, spacing
between adjacent connectors, and spacing
between connectors and adjacent shapes. To
do so, choose the Spacing button on the Layout And Routing tab. Just enter the spacing
you want for each quantity.

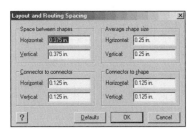

Adding Pages To A Diagram

Sometimes, despite your best efforts, all your work won't fit on one page. Visio 2000 provides the capability to add pages to a diagram, name those pages, and order them any way you want.

1.

To add a page to a diagram, select Insert|Page from the menu.

Visio 2000 displays the Page Setup dialog box where you can name the page right away, as well as adjust any of the other properties on the page.

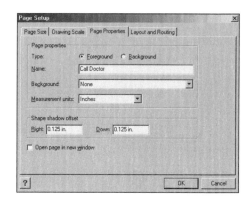

2.

Click on OK to create the new page. The page has a name tab at the bottom that displays the page's name.

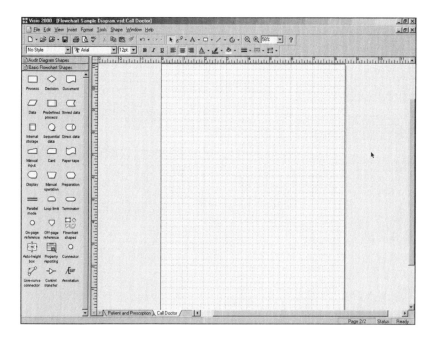

3.

To change the name of the page, double-click on the tab to make the name editable, and type a new name.

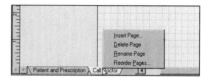

Shortcut Menu

The shortcut menu for a page enables you to insert a new page, delete the page, rename the page, or reorder the pages in the diagram.

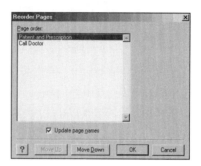

Reordering The Pages In A Diagram

If you choose to reorder the pages, the Reorder Pages dialog box opens. Click on a page name and choose the Move Up or Move Down buttons to change the page order.

Linking Pages

After you've created another page, you can create a link from one page to another using the Off-Page Reference shape.

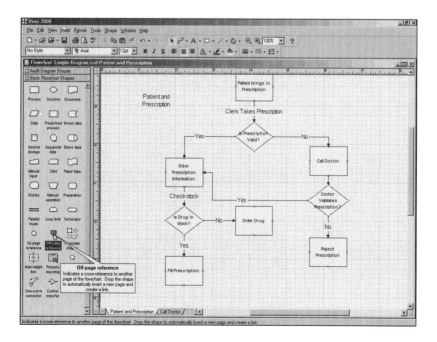

1.

Drag the Off-Page Reference shape onto a page to open the Off-Page Reference dialog box.

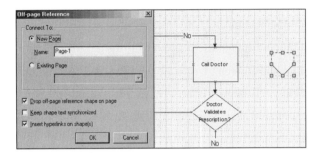

2.

Choose the Existing Page radio button and select the name of the page to which the off-page reference points.

3.

Click on OK to create the off-page reference. When you move the mouse pointer over the off-page reference, it displays the classic *hyperlink* symbol.

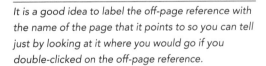

It is a good idea to label the off-page reference with the name of the page that it points to so you can tell just by looking at it where you would go if you double-clicked on the off-page reference.

4.

Double-click on the off-page reference to jump
to the page to which it points.

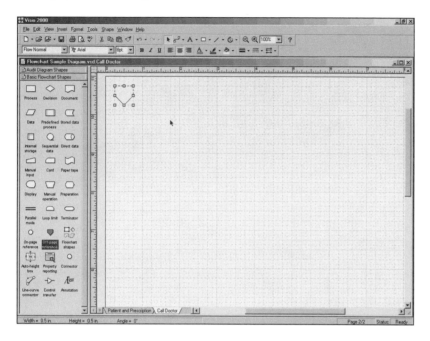

Setting Up Snap And Glue

Turning on Snap causes shapes and connecting lines to "snap" to various points, such as
ruler subdivisions, the grid, and shape connection points. Turning on Glue causes the
connecting points to become attached to a
shape at various points, such as guides or connection points.

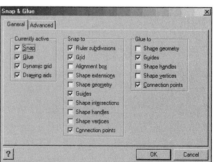

To work with Snap and Glue, select Tools|Snap
& Glue from the menu to display the Snap &
Glue dialog box.

Turning Snap Or Glue On Or Off

To turn either Snap or Glue on or off, select or
clear the checkbox in the Currently Active section of the dialog box.

Snap To Choices

To set which items lines will snap to, select or clear the checkboxes in the Snap To section.

Glue To Choices

To set which items line endpoints will glue to, select or clear the checkboxes in the Glue To section.

Snap is a handy feature for keeping items aligned in the drawing. However, you may not always want it turned on. It can often get in the way when you want to precisely position a shape or line. When it is necessary to position something exactly, turn off Snap.

Shape Geometry

One handy feature that is *not* turned on by default is the option to use Shape Geometry as both a Snap To and a Glue To. With this option turned off, the Glue feature works only on connection points (by default). Unfortunately, most shapes have only a single connection point on each side, so if you need to join two lines to the same side of the shape, they must overlap. By using the Shape Geometry option, you can glue lines to multiple points along a side. Here, the Shape Geometry option is turned on for both Snap and Glue, so multiple lines can snap and glue to the Contact Doctor rectangle.

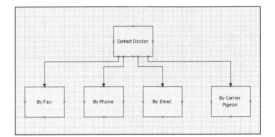

Setting Up The Ruler And Grid

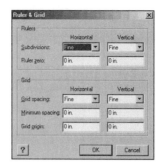

There are two rulers in Visio 2000—one along the top of the screen (horizontal), the other along the left side (vertical). You can control the precision of these rulers, as well as the size of the background grid on the page.

To adjust the ruler and grid properties, select Tools|Ruler & Grid from the menu. This opens the Ruler & Grid dialog box.

Choosing Ruler Subdivisions

For the ruler, you can choose the number of subdivisions for the horizontal and vertical rulers by selecting it from the Subdivisions drop-down menus.

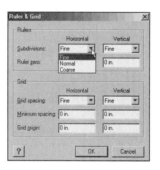

Fine And Coarse Ruler Settings

The difference between the "fine" setting on the ruler and the "coarse" setting is quite substantial, as you can see here.

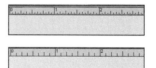

Adjusting Where Zero Appears

You can adjust the location of zero on the ruler by typing a value into the Ruler Zero field. For example, typing "2 in." into the Horizontal Ruler Zero field relocates zero to 2 inches *in* from the left side of the paper.

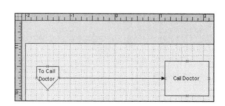

Setting Background Grid Properties

You can set the properties of the background grid from the Grid section of the Ruler & Grid dialog box. As with the ruler, you can choose a grid spacing from the Grid Spacing drop-down menus.

Setting The Minimum Spacing

The Minimum Spacing field overrides the Grid Spacing drop-down menu. For example, if you enter a minimum spacing of 1 in., the grid will have hash marks that are 1 inch apart even if the Grid Spacing drop-down menu is set to Fine.

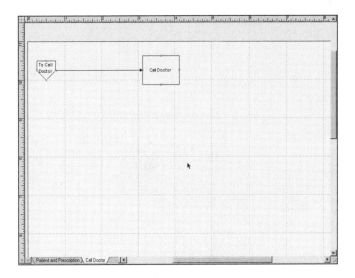

If you set the Grid Spacing drop-down menu to Fixed, you must supply a value other than zero in the Minimum Spacing field.

Setting The Color Scheme

You can apply color schemes to a drawing that changes the foreground color, background color, shadow, line color, and text color. To work with color schemes, select Tools|Color Schemes from the menu.

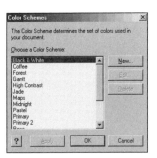

Applying An Existing Color Scheme

To apply an existing color scheme, choose a color scheme, and click on OK to apply that color scheme to the diagram. You can also click on the Apply button to apply the color scheme without closing the dialog box. You can create your own color schemes as well. The following steps show you how.

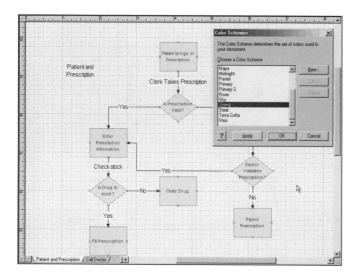

1.

Click on the New button to open the Color Scheme Details dialog box.

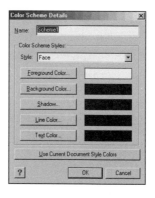

2.

Enter a name into the Name field, and if you want, click on the Use Current Document Style Colors button to start off your new color scheme with the colors in use in the current document style.

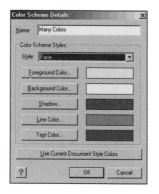

3.

To change any of the colors, click on the appropriate button (for example, the Background Color button) to display the Color dialog box.

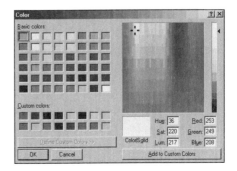

4.

Choose the color you want from the Color dialog box. Click on OK to return to the Color Schemes Details dialog box and continue customizing your color scheme until you have it just the way you want it.

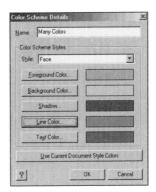

The Style drop-down menu controls which items you are setting the color for. For example, the "Face" value sets the colors for shapes, while the "Connector" value sets colors for the connectors.

5.

Click on either OK or Apply to apply the new color scheme to your drawing.

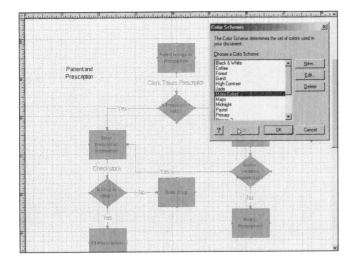

Choosing A Color Palette For The Drawing

Visio normally uses a color palette of 24 colors to draw shapes, lines, and text, as well as set background and fill colors. You can adjust these 24 colors to suit your needs.

1.

To adjust colors, select Tools|Color Palette to display the Color Palette dialog box.

To edit a color in the palette (such as color 0— the color used for shapes, lines, and text in the current drawing), choose the color and click on the Edit button.

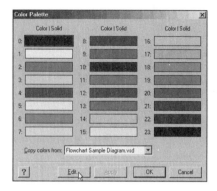

2.

Choose the color you want from the Edit Color dialog box (identical to the Color dialog box displayed in the last section), and click on OK to return to the Color Palette dialog.

Click on Apply or OK to apply your changes to the diagram.

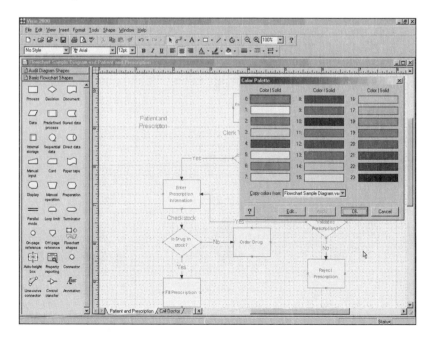

Setting A Zoom Level

You can view your Visio diagram at many different zoom (magnification) levels. High magnification enables you to do detail work, while low magnification enables you to see more of your work at once.

The easiest way to set the zoom level is to click on the Zoom drop-down menu on the toolbar.

Zoom Settings

The 100% setting shows the drawing at its actual size. You can select any of the values in this list. One of the handiest is the Page value, which zooms automatically to display the whole page in the window.

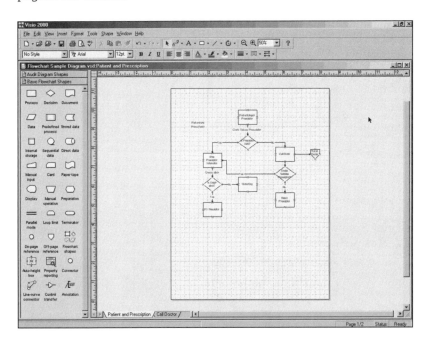

If you choose Page from the Zoom drop-down menu, Visio 2000 displays the actual zoom value (50%).

Changing Zoom Levels

You can enter a value into the drop-down menu window or click on the magnifying glass icons to increase or decrease the zoom level.

Full Screen View

The Full Screen item in the View menu displays the entire diagram without menus, stencils, or other distractions. To return to normal viewing, press the Esc key.

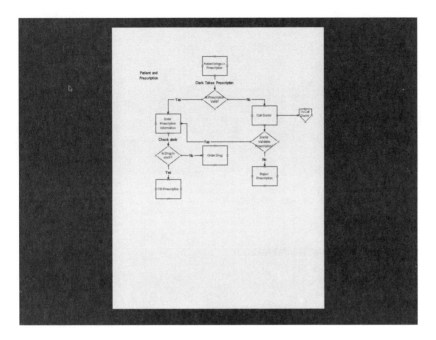

Working With Backgrounds

Visio 2000 provides the capability to use a drawing page as the background for another page.

1.

To create a page and use it as a background, select Insert|Page from the menu. In the Page Setup dialog box, choose Background as the Type, and name the page. Click on OK to create the blank page.

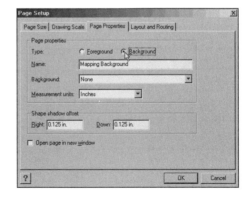

2.

Next, you need to build the background page, which you do just like any other page in Visio. However, Visio has a special stencil of backgrounds. To access this stencil, select File| Stencils|Visio Extras|Backgrounds.

3.

Choose a background shape and drag it onto the page (or build the background page some other way).

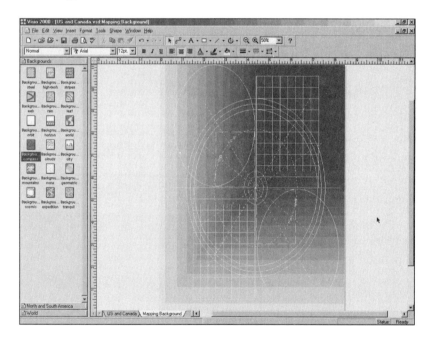

4.

Switch to the page to which you want to add
the background page.

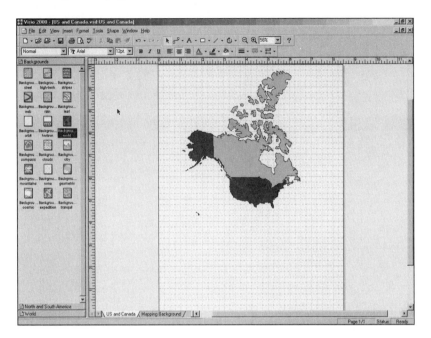

5.

Select File|Page Setup and switch to the Page
Properties tab. On the Background drop-down
menu, choose the name of the page you want
to add as a background ("Mapping Background" in this example).

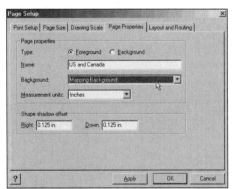

6.

Click on OK to complete the operation. The page you selected as the background now appears as the background of your main page.

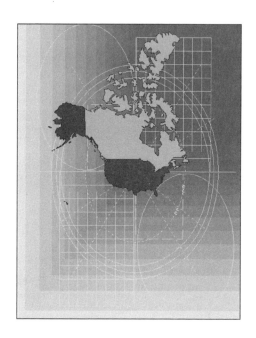

Revising The Background

Although you can't make changes to the background directly from the foreground page, you can switch to the background page and revise it. Any changes you make will also be visible on the foreground page. For example, the title added to the background page is visible near the bottom of the foreground page.

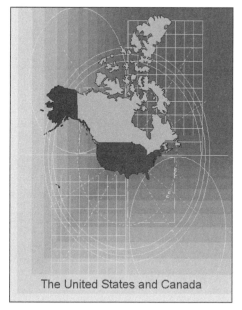

The United States and Canada

Using Headers And Footers

Visio 2000 can place text at the top of every page (Header) and at the bottom of every page (Footer). To set up the header and footer information for a page, select View|Header and Footer from the menu.

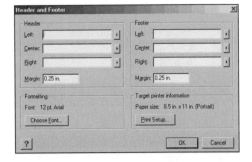

Header And Footer Options

Both the Header and Footer options are divided into three fields. You can either enter text into a field or choose a quantity (such as the date or time) from the list that appears when you click on the small arrow button to the right of each field.

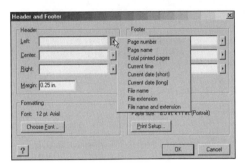

Although you choose easily recognizable items such as Page Name or Date from the menu, Visio places a code (such as &n or &d) in the actual field.

Combining Text And Menu Selections

You can choose more than one item from the list for each field and combine typed text with one or more selected items.

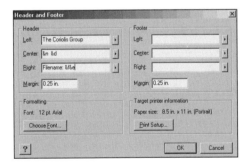

Previewing Headers And Footers

The header and footer are *not* visible in the normal page view, but you can see what they look like by switching to Print Preview mode (select File|Print Preview).

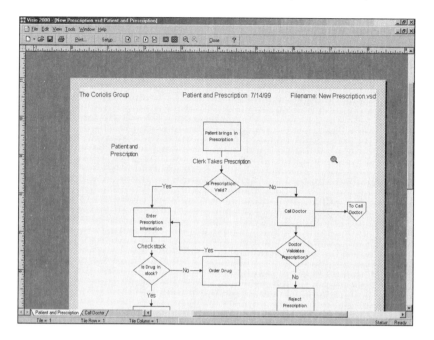

Getting The Diagram On Paper

One of the primary reasons to create a Visio 2000 diagram is so you can print it out. This section teaches you how to preview and print your drawing. The following steps walk you through printing a diagram.

1.

To print a Visio 2000 drawing, select File|Print. This opens the Print dialog box.

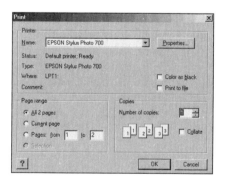

2.

Select the printer you want to use from the
Name drop-down menu. Your list of printers
will look different depending on the printers
you have installed.

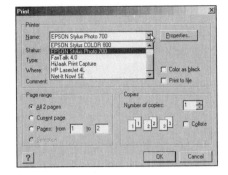

3.

In the Page Range section, choose which pages
you want to print.

4.

Choose the number of copies you want and
whether to collate multiple copies in the Copies section. Then, click on OK to Print.

Previewing The Page
You can preview what the page will look like before printing by choosing File|Print Preview.

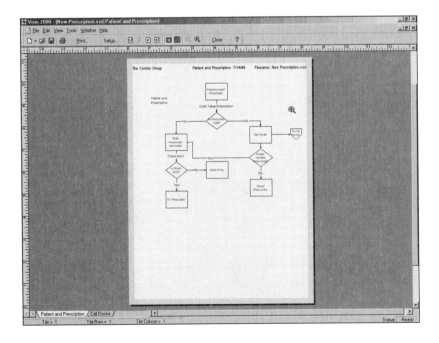

Zooming In On Preview Pages

To toggle the zoom level up (higher magnification) click on the diagram with the "plus" magnifying glass; to toggle back down (lower magnification) click on the diagram with the "minus" magnifying glass.

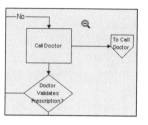

Stepping Through Preview Pages

You can also step through multiple pages using the Tile buttons on the toolbar.

Adjusting Other Print Options

To adjust other printing options, click on the Setup button on the Print Preview window toolbar. This displays the Page Setup dialog box (also available from the File menu) with the Print Setup tab displayed.

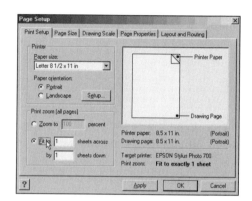

From here, you can set the paper size and orientation and set the print zoom level for all pages. For example, you can choose to fit a large diagram onto a specified number of pages across and down.

Chapter 5
Changing Basic Shape And Line Properties

- Learn to format shapes by resizing and changing the fill color and pattern

- Change line color, pattern, and the details of the line ends

- Modify shapes by resizing them and duplicating lines and shapes

- Align and layer shapes on the page

- Flip and rotate shapes

- Group shapes so they move and size as one shape

Manipulating Shapes And Lines

In this chapter you will learn to manipulate shapes and lines by changing their color, pattern, fill, and line ends. You'll align multiple shapes, arrange them in layers, and flip and rotate shapes. You will group shapes into a single shape, making them easier to use as a unit.

Modifying The Shape Outline

The following section teaches you how to modify the outline of the shape. Select File|New|Block Diagram|Basic Diagram to start a diagram to practice the examples in this chapter.

1.

Drag two Rectangle shapes onto the basic diagram and join them with a connector.

To modify the shape outline, select Format|Line from the main menu or the shape's shortcut menu.

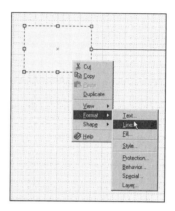

2.

This opens the Line dialog box.

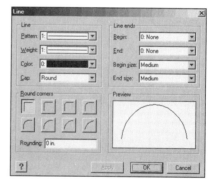

3.

To change the shape outline, choose a value from each of the Pattern, Weight, and Color drop-down menus. For example, choose Pattern 7, Weight 9, and Color 4.

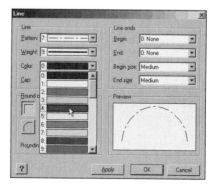

4.

To round the corners of the shape, choose one of the buttons in the Round Corners section. For example, select the third button from the left in the top row.

Click on Apply or OK to implement the changes to the shape.

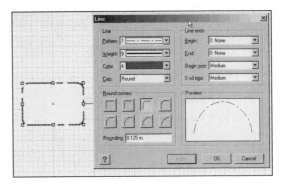

If you don't like any of the preset rounding radius corners, enter your own value in the Rounding field.

Resizing A Shape

To resize a shape, use the sizing *handles*—the small green squares displayed around the shape's perimeter. Click and drag one of the sizing handles to change the size of the shape.

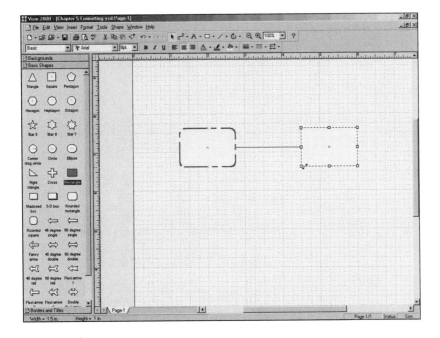

Modifying Fill Properties And Color

The following steps teach you how to modify the shape's fill color and pattern. Continue to use your basic diagram.

1.

Select Format|Fill from the main menu or the shape's shortcut menu. This opens the Fill dialog box.

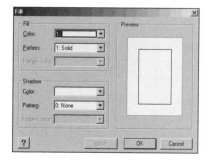

2.

To modify the fill, choose a color, pattern, and pattern color. For example, choose Color 4, Pattern 17, and Pattern Color 7.

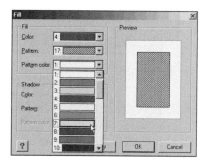

3.

Click on Apply or OK to implement your changes to the shape.

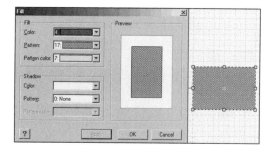

4.

You can choose the color, pattern, and pattern color for the shape's shadow from the Fill dialog box as well. Or, you can select Format|Shadow from the menu to display the Shadow dialog box.

If you don't like the standard colors listed in the color drop-down menu, select Custom. This opens the Edit Color dialog box.

Modifying Connecting Line Color And Style

The following steps teach you how to modify the properties of a connecting line. Continue to use your basic diagram.

1.

Select Format|Line from the menu or the line's shortcut menu. This opens the Line dialog box, which is identical to the Line dialog box for a shape. All the options on the left side of the dialog box (pattern, weight, color, Round corners) work the same as well.

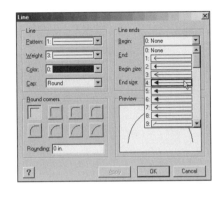

To change the details of the line ends, use the drop-down menus in the Line Ends section. For example, choose 4 from the Begin drop-down menu.

2.

Choose 10 from the End drop-down menu.

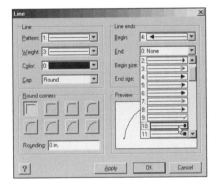

3.

Choose Large from the Begin Size drop-down menu.

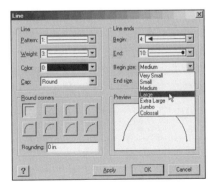

4.

Choose Colossal from the End Size drop-down menu. Then click on OK or Apply to implement your changes to the line.

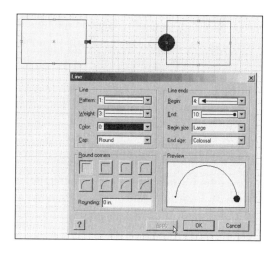

Duplicating Objects

In the following steps, you will practice duplicating objects. Continue to use your basic diagram.

1.

The simplest way to make an exact copy of an object is to select the object and choose Duplicate from the Edit menu or from the object's shortcut menu.

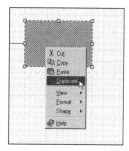

2.

This action creates a copy near the original object. Unfortunately, you can't control exactly where the new copy will appear. You can also only create a single copy each time you click on Duplicate.

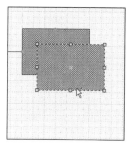

3.

If you need to make multiple copies, it is more efficient to select the object and choose Copy from the Edit menu or the object's shortcut menu.

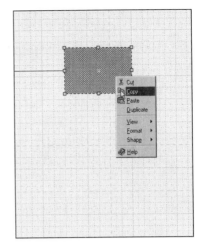

4.

Then, choose Paste from the Edit menu or the drawing's shortcut menu.

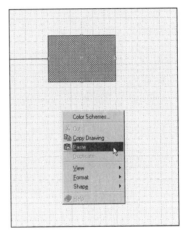

5.

This pastes a copy of the shape into the diagram; you can make multiple copies by continually clicking and pasting.

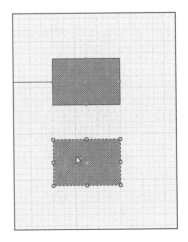

Working With Multiple Shapes

It can be very handy to work with multiple shapes. You can move multiple shapes as a single unit, group them together into a single shape, align the shapes, and even stack them in the order you want. This section discusses how to select multiple shapes and perform multishape operations.

Selecting Multiple Shapes

In the following steps, you will practice selecting multiple shapes. Continue to use your basic diagram.

1.

The first step in working with multiple shapes is to select them. The easiest way to select multiple shapes is to drag a rectangle around the shapes.

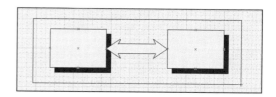

2.

This selects all the shapes inside the rectangle.

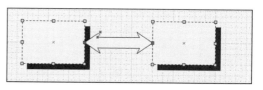

3.

Another way to select multiple shapes is to click on the first shape, hold down the Shift key, and click on the other shapes you want. You need to use this technique if the shapes you want to select are not arranged in such a way that you can drag a rectangle around them.

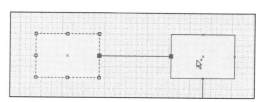

If you accidentally select a shape that you don't want, shift-click on it again and Visio will deselect it. You can also drag a rectangle around a group of shapes to select them, and shift-click any of the selected shapes to deselect them.

Aligning Shapes

In the following steps, you will practice aligning multiple shapes. Continue to use your basic diagram.

1.

You can align multiple shapes on any edge or centerline. Select the shapes you want to align. The first shape you should select is the one to which you want the other shapes to align. Once selected, this shape displays green handles and the additional shapes display blue handles.

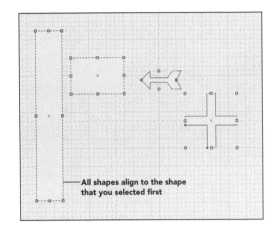

All shapes align to the shape that you selected first

2.

Select Tools|Align Shapes to display the Align Shapes dialog box. Note the following buttons:

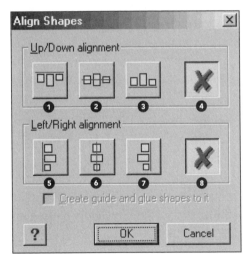

1. Align to top edges

2. Align to vertical centerlines

3. Align to bottom edges

4. Remove up/down alignment

5. Align to left edges

6. Align to horizontal centerlines

7. Align to right edges

8. Remove left/right alignment

3.

Choose the top-left button (align to top edges) and click on OK to apply the alignment.

Notice that the arrow in the graphic aligns to its horizontal centerline, despite your choice of aligning to top edges. This is because the arrow is a connector object; connector objects always align to their centerlines (either horizontal or vertical, depending on whether you choose to align up/down or left/right).

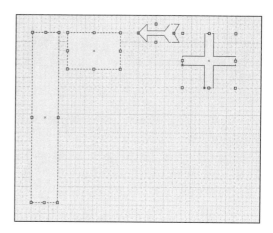

4.

You can also use Visio 2000's guides to perform alignments. The advantage of this technique is, if you move the guide, the shapes move with it. Try this by reselecting all the shapes, and once again make sure that the first shape you select is the one to which you want the others to align. Then select Tools|Align Shapes, click on the Align to bottom edges button, and place a checkmark in the Create Guide And Glue Shapes To It checkbox.

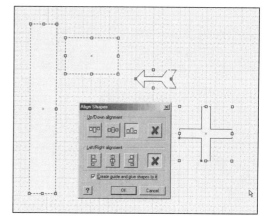

5.

Click on OK. The shapes align to their bottom edges, and Visio 2000 provides a horizontal guide.

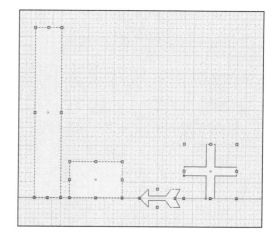

6.

Click on the guide and drag it to a new position.

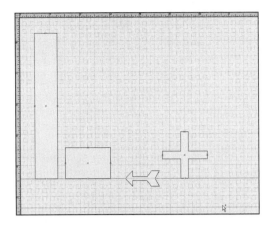

7.

Release the guide. Notice how the shapes remain aligned and move with the guide. (Compare the position of the shapes and guide with the vertical ruler in this graphic and the previous one.)

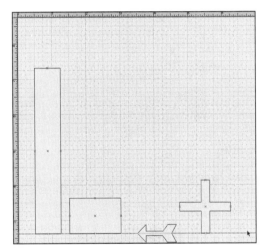

Distributing Shapes

Visio 2000 can evenly distribute the shapes in a drawing across a specified area. Continue to use your basic diagram to practice this technique in the following steps.

1.

To align the shapes, select the shapes you want to work with.

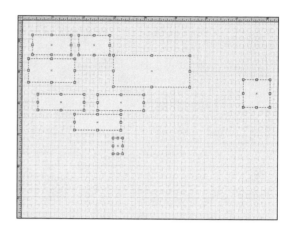

2.

Select Tools|Distribute Shapes to open the Distribute Shapes dialog box. Note the following buttons:

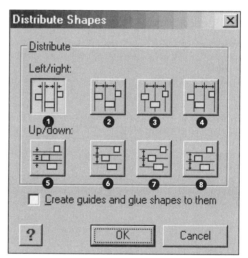

1. Distribute by distance between adjacent edges

2. Distribute by distance between left edges

3. Distribute by distance between vertical centerlines

4. Distribute by distance between right edges

5. Distribute by distance between top/ bottom

6. Distribute by distance between top edges

7. Distribute by distance between horizontal centerlines

8. Distribute by distance between bottom edges

3.

The buttons allow both left/right and up/down distribution. Choose the distribute by vertical centerlines button (second from right in the left/right section); then click on OK. The selected shapes are distributed evenly across the space between the left-most and right-most shapes.

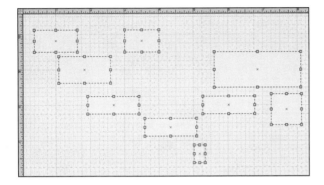

4.

You can also use Visio 2000's guides to perform distributions. After the distribution takes place, several guides are available for you to move the shapes while maintaining the spatial relationships between them. Try this by selecting the shapes you want to distribute.

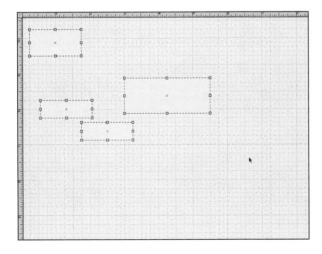

5.

Select Tools|Distribute Shapes and choose the second button from the left in the up/down section (distribute by top edges). Then select the Create Guides And Glue Shapes To Them checkbox.

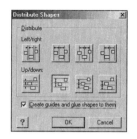

6.

Click on OK. Visio 2000 performs the distribution and provides a guide along the top edge of each shape. The guide appears along the top edge because you performed a distribution by top edges.

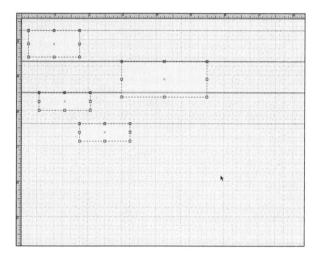

7.

Click on one of the guides, and drag it toward the bottom of the page. All the shapes move toward the bottom of the page, maintaining their relative distance.

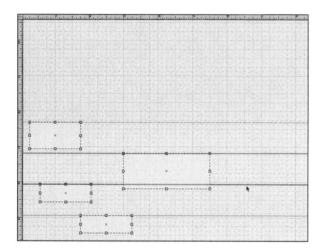

Arranging Shapes

When you place shapes in a drawing, each shape has a stacking order. The default stacking order is the order in which you add the shapes to the diagram. Shapes added later are "higher" in order (and will obstruct the view of previously added shapes) than shapes added earlier. The rectangles illustrated here were added to the diagram in the order indicated by their number.

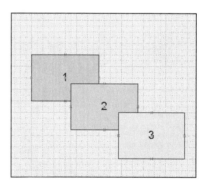

1.

You can change the stacking order of the shapes. To do so, right-click on the shape whose stacking order you want to change, and select either Shape|Send To Back or Shape|Bring To Front from the shortcut menu.

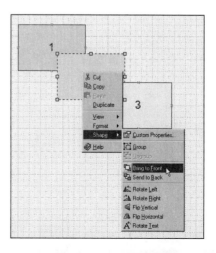

2.

For example, if you select Shape|Send To Back from the shortcut menu for shape 2, it ends up at the bottom of the stack, behind shapes 1 and 3.

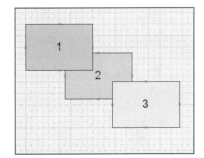

3.

You can also move shapes up or down one level at a time. To see this, let's add a large rounded rectangle to the diagram that obscures all the rectangles.

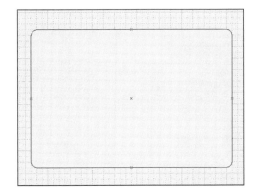

4.

Click on the rounded rectangle and select Shape|Send Backward from the main menu. This sends the rounded rectangle down one level, exposing rectangle 3.

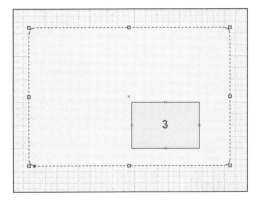

5.

If you repeat this action, rectangle 1 is exposed as well.

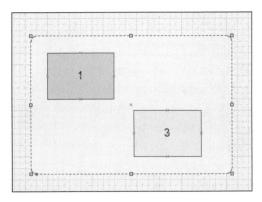

Flipping And Rotating Shapes

You can flip shapes at any 90-degree angle or rotate a shape at any angle. To flip a shape, right-click on the shape and choose one of the flip or rotate commands in the shortcut menu (these are also available in the main Shape menu).

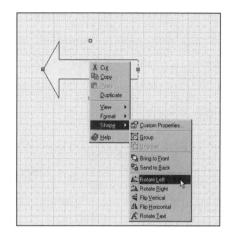

1.

As an example, choose Rotate Left and note the change to the selected shape.

2.

To rotate a shape by any angle, select the shape and choose the Rotation tool from the toolbar.

3.

Place the rotation tool over one of the rotation handles. (These handles are round as opposed to the square sizing handles.) The mouse cursor turns into a rotation cursor when you place it over a rotation handle.

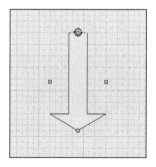

4.

Drag the rotation handle and watch as the shape rotates in the direction you choose.

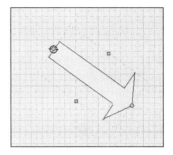

Using The Center Of Rotation

Some shapes (such as the rectangle in this example) have a center of rotation in addition to rotation handles. The center of rotation looks like a tiny circle with plus (+) symbol in it.

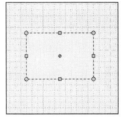

1.

You can drag the center of rotation to a new position with the mouse.

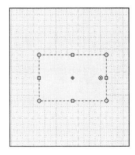

2.

Once you've relocated the center of rotation, dragging one of the rotation handles rotates the shape around the new center of rotation.

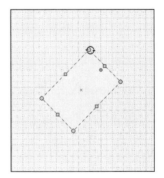

Grouping Shapes

You can group a set of Visio shapes together, which enables you to move and size the shapes as a single shape.

1.

Try this by opening the Forms Shapes stencil (File|Stencils|Forms and Charts|Forms Shapes) and drag a few shapes from the stencil onto a blank page. To follow along with the example, make sure one of the shapes is a Name/Address block, and also drag some checkboxes (see the graphic).

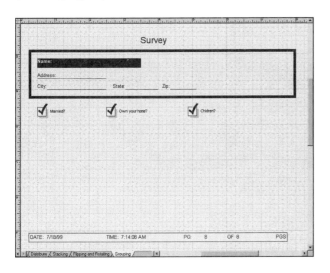

2.

Select all the items in the Name/Address block
by dragging a rectangle around them.

Select Shape|Grouping|Group from the menu.

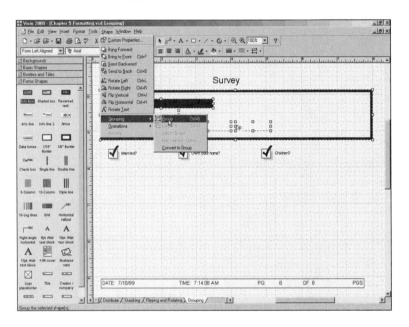

3.

Notice how all the shapes are now treated as
a group. Click on the shape and drag it to a
new location below the checkmarks. All the
objects move together.

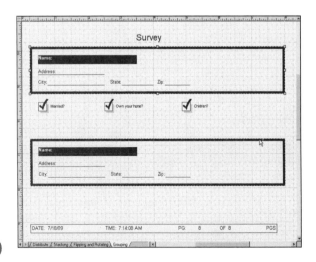

4.

Click on the sizing handle in the lower-right corner and drag it to make the shape smaller. All of the objects included in the shape shrink together.

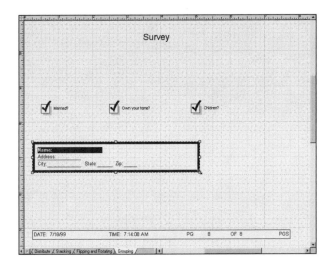

5.

Even though you have grouped these shapes together, you can still control the individual shapes that make up the group. To see this, click on the Zip code field once, which selects the group, and click again to select the actual Zip code field.

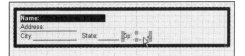

6.

Now you can drag or resize the Zip code field *within* the group.

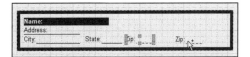

7.

You can even remove a single object (such as the Zip code field) from a group by selecting the single object within the group and selecting Shape|Grouping|Remove From Group.

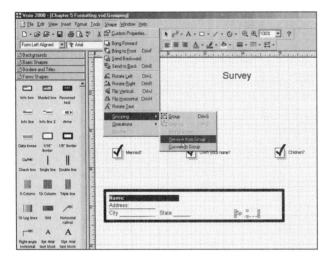

8.

If you want to add an object to an existing group, select the group and the object(s), then select Shape|Grouping|Add To Group. Or, to return the shapes in a group to their original, ungrouped condition, choose the group and select Shape|Grouping|Ungroup. The items are now individual shapes again.

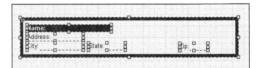

Chapter 6
Working With Text

- Rotate text in a drawing

- Learn to set the text properties:
  color, font, and effects

- Set the paragraph properties:
  alignment, bullets, and tabs

- Learn to use the spell checker

Going Beyond Plain Text

Text is a very important part of a Visio drawing. It is used to identify shapes, explain portions of the drawing, and provide notes. You are not limited to just typing plain text in the drawing. Visio allows you to format the text in many ways, changing just about every property of the text to suit the diagram style. This chapter teaches you how to work with text properties, rotate text, and spellcheck your text.

Rotating Text

As you learned in Chapter 5, you can rotate a shape either in 90-degree increments or by any arbitrary angle. You can also rotate text in much the same way—both text within shapes and text blocks.

Rotating And Moving Text Within A Shape

The following exercise will help you practice rotating and moving text within a shape.

1.

Create a new Basic Flowchart drawing (File| New|Flowchart|Basic Flowchart). Drop a Pro- cess shape on the drawing and type in "Clerk Enters Personal Information" to provide some text to work with. Click and drag one of the sizing handles on the right edge of the rect- angle to make it long and thin—long enough for all the text to fit on one line.

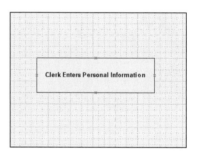

2.

Right-click on the shape and select Shape|Rotate Text from the shortcut menu.

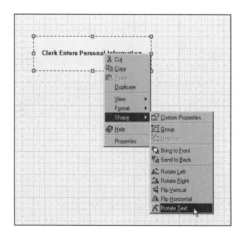

3.

The text rotates counterclockwise *without* affecting the orientation of the shape. Each time you select this menu option, the text rotates counterclockwise by 90 degrees.

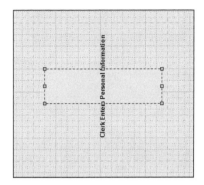

4.

You can also rotate the text within a shape using any arbitrary angle without changing the shape orientation. To do so, choose the Text Block tool from the toolbar.

5.

Move the cursor over one of the rotation handles (the round handles that appear at each corner of the text's rectangle).

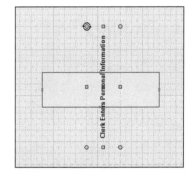

6.

Drag the rotation handle and the text rotates to any angle.

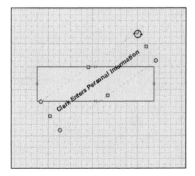

7.

You can also relocate the shape's text. To do so, move the Text Block tool anywhere inside the text's rectangle. It turns into a double-rectangle shape.

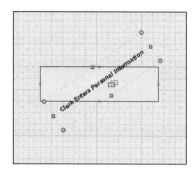

8.

Click and drag the mouse. As you can see, the text moves with the mouse; you can even drag the text outside the shape.

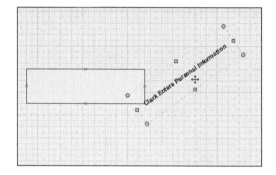

Rotating A Text Block

In the following exercise, you will rotate a text block.

1.

To work with a text block, choose the Text tool from the toolbar.

2.

Drag a rectangle into the drawing using the Text tool to create the text block.

3.

Type some text into the text block.

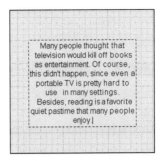

4.

You can rotate and move the text in a text block in exactly the same way as you can in any other shape. For example, select the text block, and then select Shape|Rotate Text from the shortcut menu to rotate the text 90 degrees counterclockwise.

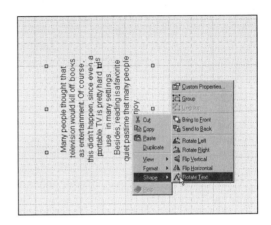

Be careful to select the text block, and not the text in the text block. If you accidentally select the text in the text block, the shortcut menu you see when you right-click is the shortcut menu for text—it does not include an option to rotate the text.

5.

You can also rotate the text to any angle or drag it with the Text Block tool.

6.

In addition, you can work directly with the text block shape, modifying the shape instead of the text in the shape. Because the text block does not have visible boundaries, the effect is the same. Click on the Rotation tool.

7.

Drag the center of rotation to a new location, such as the upper-left corner of the text block.

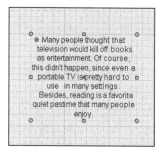

8.

As with any other shape, the text block now rotates around the new center of rotation.

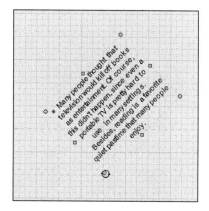

Modifying Text Properties

You can modify the properties of any text; it doesn't matter if the text is inside a shape or is in a text block. The toolbars provide tools for modifying the text properties, and Visio 2000 contains a comprehensive dialog box for making changes as well. This section shows you how to modify the text to look just the way you want.

Selecting The Text

Obviously, you must tell Visio which text you want to modify. Depending on what you are trying to achieve, there are two methods for selecting text. In the following steps, you'll practice both methods for selecting text.

1.

The first method is to simply select the shape (or text block) that contains the text.

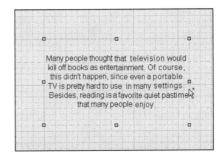

2.

When you make changes to the text, all the text in the shape or text block is affected by the change. For example, you can click on the Bold button on the toolbar to boldface all the text in the shape.

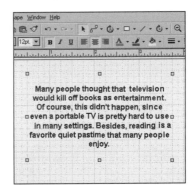

3.

The second method of selecting text is to highlight the portion of the text you want to modify within the shape or text block. Using the Text tool, click and drag the I-beam cursor over the text you want to change.

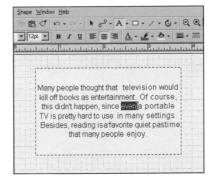

4.

Now you can apply changes to the highlighted text from the toolbar, Text dialog box, or the shortcut menu. For example, you could click on the Italic button on the toolbar to italicize the selected word.

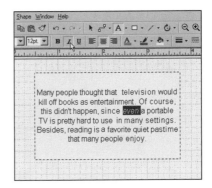

Making Changes From The Toolbar And Menus

The toolbar provides a variety of buttons and drop-down menus to modify text. Practice using these techniques in the following steps.

1.

To make some modifications, choose a shape with some text in it (a text block will work also) and click on the list of fonts.

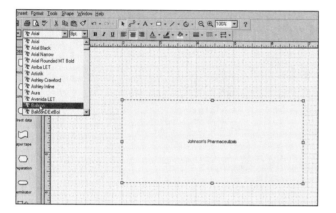

2.

Choose the Balloon font (or another font if you don't have the Balloon font).

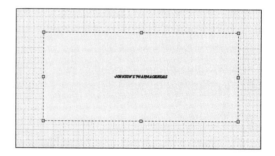

3.

Click on the drop-down menu of font sizes.

4.

Choose 18 pt. from the list.

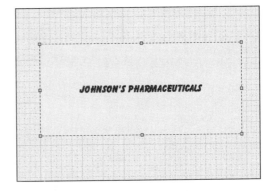

5.

The three buttons to the right of the font size list on the Format toolbar enable you to add bold, italic, or underline styles to the text. Click on all three buttons to modify the text.

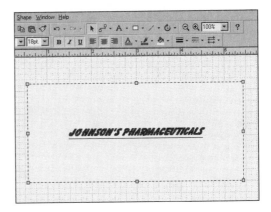

6.

The next three buttons to the right on the Format toolbar change the alignment of the text. Click on the Align Left button to align the text to the left side of the shape (or the text block boundary).

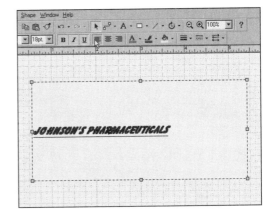

7.

Click on the drop arrow alongside the font color button and choose a color for the text.

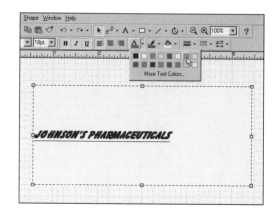

8.

The color of the text changes to match the color you selected.

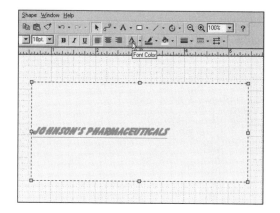

Using The Text Shortcut Menu

The shortcut menu offers a variety of options for modifying text.

1.

If you select the text in a shape or text block, you can right-click on the selected text to display the text shortcut menu.

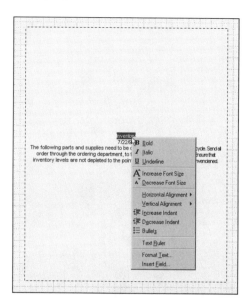

2.

To demonstrate the use of the various options on the text shortcut menu, create an inventory form as shown in the next figure. Use a Process shape and type in the text. Use Arial 10 pt. font.

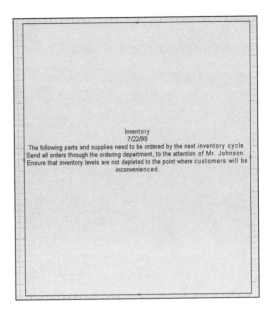

3.

Highlight the word "Inventory" and choose Bold from the shortcut menu. Then choose Increase Font Size.

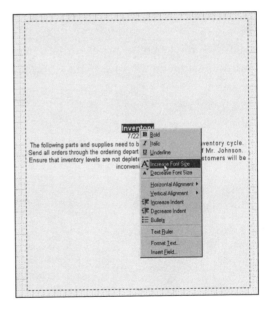

4.

Highlight the date and select Horizontal Alignment|Left from the shortcut menu.

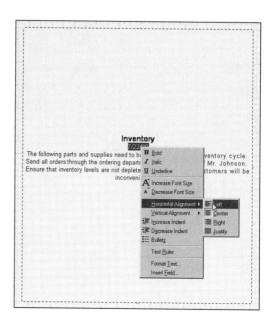

5.

Right-click anywhere in the text and select Vertical Alignment|Top from the shortcut menu.

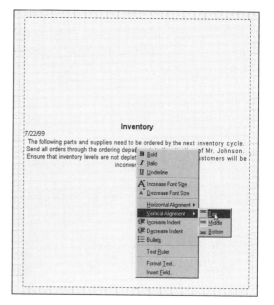

6.

This moves all the text to the top of the form.

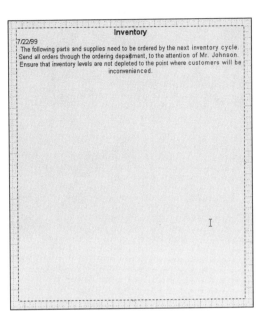

7.

Place the text cursor after the last word, press Enter twice, and type "Approved by (Assistant Manager)". Press Enter and type "Approved by (Manager)". Highlight these two lines and select Horizontal Alignment|Left from the shortcut menu.

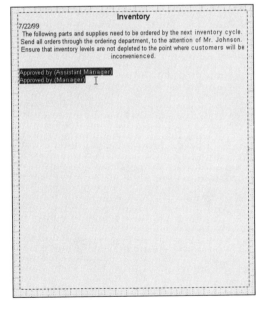

8.

Right-click on the two approval lines and choose Increase Indent from the shortcut menu. This indents the two lines from the left edge of the shape.

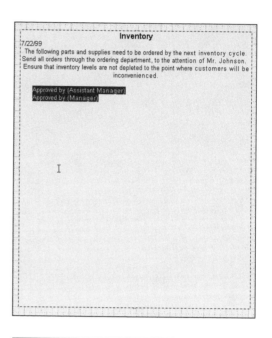

9.

Place the cursor after the last character and press Enter three times. Type in a list of inventory items to order.

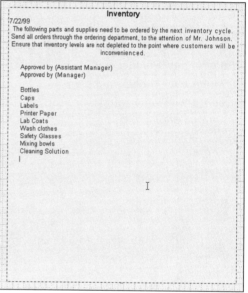

10.

Highlight all the inventory items, and choose Bullets from the shortcut menu.

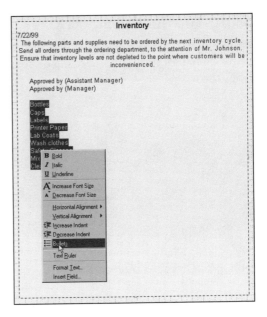

11.

The items in the list now have bullets alongside them. To make things neater, choose Increase Indent from the shortcut menu to indent the bulleted list.

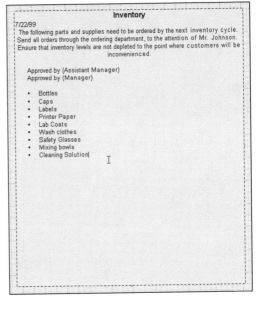

Using The Text Dialog Box

Next, you're going to format the text in the following shape using a specialized dialog box.

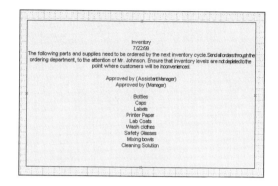

1.

To activate the Text dialog box, highlight the word Inventory in the diagram and choose Format Text from the shortcut menu.

You can also select a shape and choose Format/Text from the shortcut menu.

2.

You can choose the font and size from the Font drop-down menu and the Size drop-down menu, just as you can from the toolbar. In this example, choose Arial 14 pt.

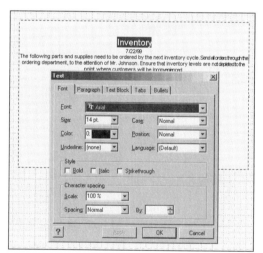

3.

To change the color of the selected text, click on the Color drop-down menu and choose a color. In this example, choose color 6.

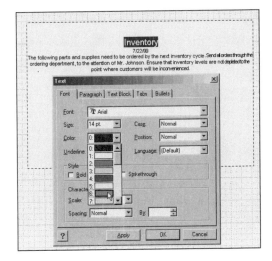

4.

You can choose a single or double underline from the Underline drop-down menu. In this case, choose the double-underline.

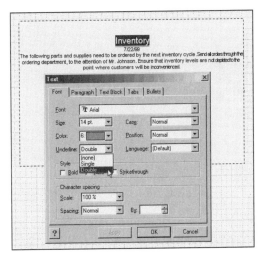

5.

To change the Case of the text (All Caps, Initial Caps, and so on), make your selection from the Case drop-down menu. For this example, choose All Caps.

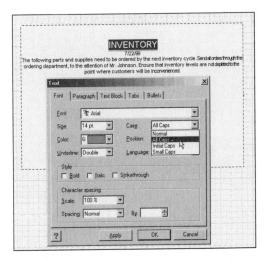

6.

To specify the text as superscript or subscript, make your choice from the Position drop-down menu.

7.

Select the Bold and Italic checkboxes in the Style section of the dialog box to format "Inventory" using those styles. Click on OK to apply all the changes.

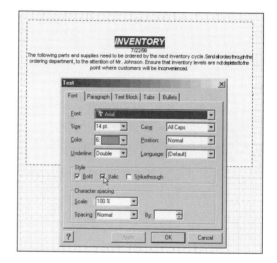

8.

Highlight the rest of the text in the shape, right-click on the selected text, and choose Format Text from the shortcut menu. Choose Arial 12 pt. for the font size.

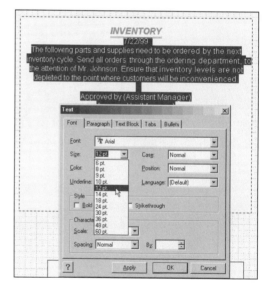

9.

Click on OK to activate the changes. Highlight the two "Approved by" lines and activate the Text dialog box again. Click on the Paragraph tab and choose Left from the Horizontal Alignment drop-down menu.

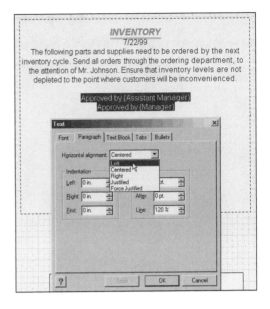

10.

In the Indentation section, set a Left indentation of 0.3 in. using the spinner control.

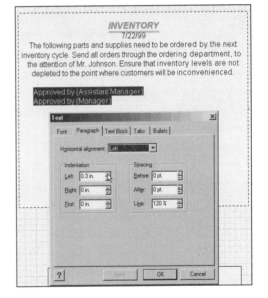

11.

In the Spacing section, set an extra 6 pt. spacing before and after the selected lines. Click on OK to apply the changes.

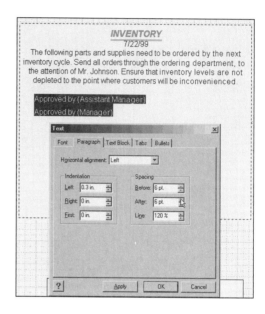

12.

Next, highlight the paragraph just below "Inventory" and choose a Horizontal Alignment of Justified. You can do this either by using the Paragraph tab of the Text dialog box, or by selecting Justify from the text shortcut menu. This extends the text from margin to margin, except for the last line.

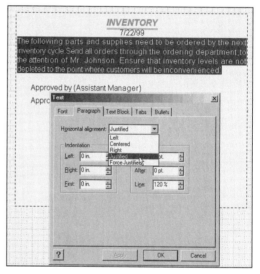

13.

The Text Block tab works a little differently from the other tabs, because it applies to the entire block of text, *not* just to the text you have selected.

14.

Set a top margin of 18 pt., a Left Margin of 20 pt., and a Right Margin of 20 pt.

There are 72 points in an inch.

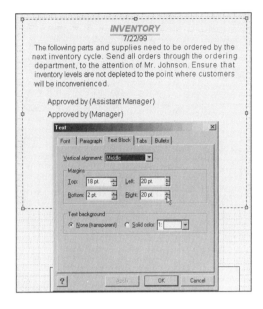

15.

You can also change the background color for the text block by choosing a color from the Solid Color drop-down menu. Click on OK to apply the changes.

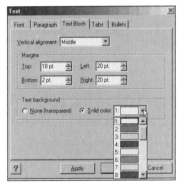

16.

Highlight the list of items (Bottles, Caps, and so on), return to the Text dialog box, and choose the Bullets tab.

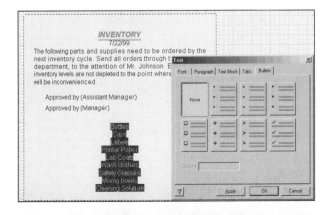

17.

Choose a bullet style and click on Apply. This
example applies the bullets and left justifies
the list of items.

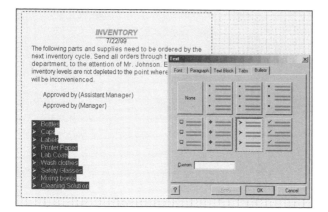

Using Tabs In The Text Dialog Box

The last tab in the Text dialog box is the Tabs
tab. To see how this works, create a shape and
type in the text as shown in the next graphic.
Be sure to begin each line by pressing the Tab
key and press Tab after each piece of data.

1.

Right-click on the shape and select Format|Text
from the shortcut menu. Click on the Tabs tab
of the Text dialog box that appears.

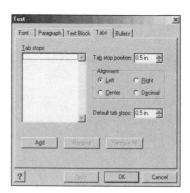

2.

Click on the Add button to add a 0.5 in. Left aligned tab (the radio button in the Alignment section is set to Left).

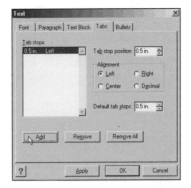

3.

Click on Add again to create the next tab. Use the Tab Stop Position spinner to set the tab to 2.5 in. As you change the value in the spinner, the value of the currently selected tab in the Tab Stops list changes to match. Choose Decimal from the Alignment section so that the decimal points of the quantities will line up.

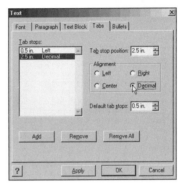

4.

Add a 3.5 in. Left tab, then click on OK to apply the changes. Notice how the resulting text now lines up nicely in the shape.

Using The Spell Checker

Visio comes with a spell checker so you can check the spelling of any text you place in a diagram. With the spell checker, you can spellcheck a page, your entire drawing, or just the selected text.

1.

To activate the spell checker, select Tools|Spelling.

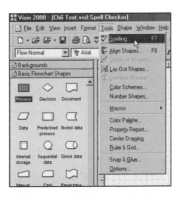

133

2.

The spell checker immediately begins checking your words, flagging the first word it doesn't recognize.

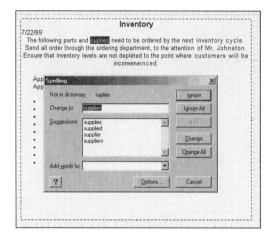

3.

However, if you haven't configured the Spell Checker, you should click on the Options button to bring up the Options dialog box for the Spelling tool.

4.

In the Search section, choose whether to spellcheck just the selected text or object, the current Page, or All Pages in the drawing.

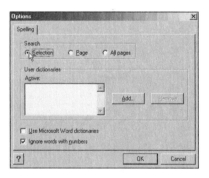

5.

If you haven't added a User dictionary (for storing words not included with the base dictionary), click on the Add button. This displays the Add User Dictionary dialog box.

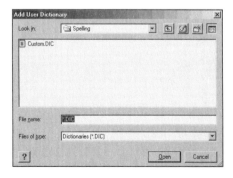

6.

Choose an existing User dictionary (the dictionary Custom.DIC is supplied with Visio) and click on Open. Click on OK to return to the Spelling tool.

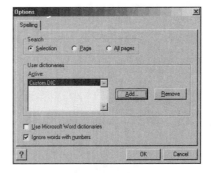

7.

As Visio 2000 encounters each misspelled word, it suggests a list of possible corrections with the most likely suggestion placed in the Change To field.

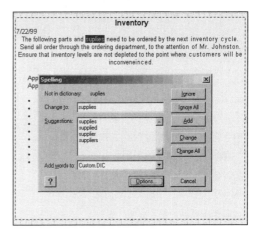

8.

To accept the suggestion in the Change To field, click on the Change button (to change this occurrence of the misspelled word) or the Change All button (to change all occurrences of this misspelled word).

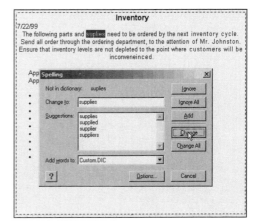

9.

You can also choose the Ignore button, which ignores this misspelled word but does *not* add it to the dictionary. You might use this option (or the Ignore All option) if the word is unusual and you don't expect to encounter it again.

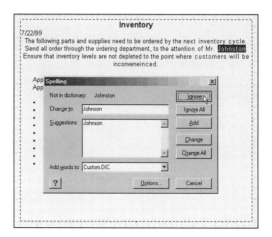

10.

To add a word to the custom dictionary, click on the Add button. For example, if you will be communicating about Mr. Johnston a lot, so you'll want to add his name to the User dictionary.

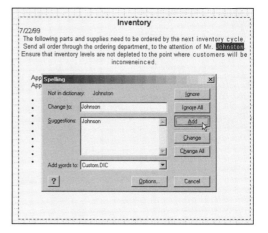

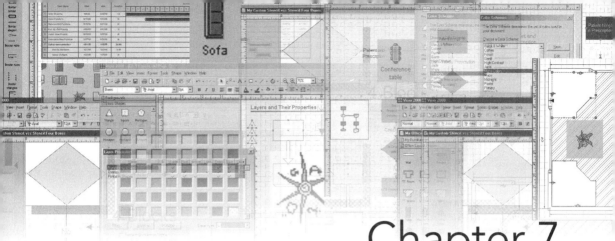

Chapter 7
Advanced Shape Editing

- Learn to define, modify, display, and summarize custom properties

- Apply, modify, and create formatting styles for shapes, lines, and text

- Number shapes, both manually and automatically

- Merge shapes, modify shape behavior, and control shape attributes

- Add graphics and clip art to drawings and modify the graphics

- Add hyperlinks to shapes so you can jump to another page, an application document, or a Web site

Doing Much More With Visio

You can do much more with Visio 2000, and this chapter introduces you to some of the product's useful capabilities. For example, you can define your own data about a shape with custom properties. You can apply formatting styles to shapes, lines, and text—changing the style, which then changes the properties of everything that uses that style. You are not limited to the shapes provided by Visio 2000; you can combine shapes using operations such as Union and Combine to create new shapes. And, you can use a Visio 2000 shape as a link to another page, a document created in another application, or a Web site.

Working With Custom Properties

You can record data about a shape or a line in Visio 2000. Such data might include the owner of a piece of office furniture, the physical location of a network node, or the estimated execution time of a process. This data is called *custom properties*. Visio 2000 predefines some custom properties for certain shapes, however, you can modify the custom properties and create your own.

Defining And Changing Custom Properties

To follow along with this example, create a new drawing from the Office Layout template (File|New|Office Layout|Office Layout). Then, drag the rectangular room onto the diagram, place a printer in the upper-right corner, and a desk and PC next to it—as shown in the first graphic.

1.

To view the custom properties for an item, right-click on the item (such as the printer) and choose Properties from the shortcut menu.

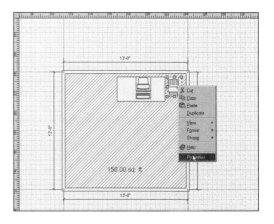

2.

This displays the Custom Properties dialog box in which you can indicate quantities for the custom properties.

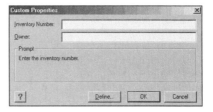

3.

Alternatively, you can highlight the item and select View|Windows|Custom Properties to view the Custom Properties window.

4.

To fill in values for the Custom Properties, just type them into either the Custom Properties dialog box or the Custom Properties window.

5.

You aren't limited to the predefined custom properties—you can create your own. To do so, right-click in the main area of the Custom Properties window and choose Define Properties from the shortcut menu. Alternatively, click on the Define button in the Custom Properties dialog box.

6.

Either way, Visio 2000 opens the Define Custom Properties dialog box.

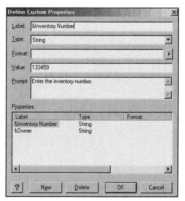

7.

The Properties section at the bottom of the dialog box lists all the custom properties. To select a different one, click on the Custom Property in the Properties section. You can then modify any of the quantities. For example, change the Prompt to make it more helpful.

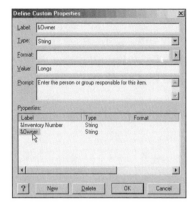

8.

To create new custom properties, click on the New button. This adds a new custom property with a default name.

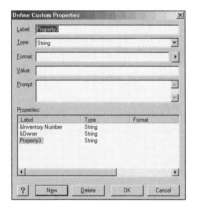

9.

Change the name by typing a new name into the Label field. In the example, type in "Pages Per Minute" for the Printer.

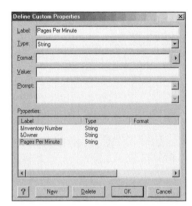

10.

Next choose the data type from the Type drop-down menu. In the example, choose Number.

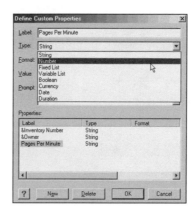

11.

Choose the format for the data from the Format field. To use a predefined format, click on the arrow to the right of the Format field window.

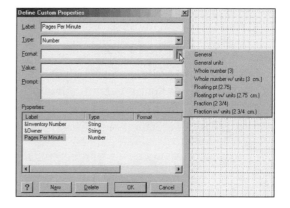

12.

Visio 2000 translates the selected format into special characters and places those characters in the Format field. In the example, I chose General, which placed the "#" symbols in the field.

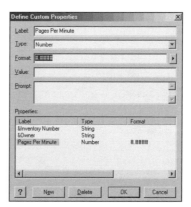

13.

The values available in the Format field vary depending on the type you select in the Type field. For example, if you create a custom property called "Date Obtained" and choose a Date type, the Formats available correspond to various date types.

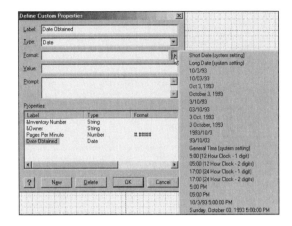

14.

If you wish, you can add a value now, or you can add it later using the Custom Properties dialog box or Custom Properties window. To display a prompt that reminds you what the data field is for, enter the prompt in the Prompt field.

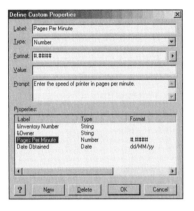

15.

Click on OK to complete the changes. Notice that the fields are available in the Custom Properties dialog box and in the Custom Properties window.

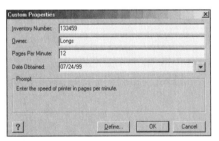

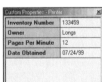

Fixed And Variable List Fields

Two of the types listed in the Type field need further explanation: Fixed List and Variable List. To see how these useful types work, follow these steps.

1.

Right-click on the PC item from the previous exercise. Choose Properties from the shortcut menu, click on the Define button, and then click on New. Enter the Label as CPU, and choose Variable List in the Type field.

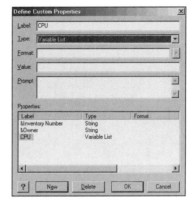

2.

In the Format field, enter the possible valid values for the CPU type separating the values with semicolons: "486;Pentium;Pentium II;Pentium III;K6-2;K6-3;Alpha".

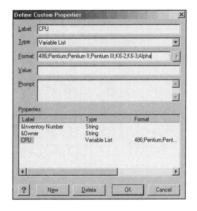

The difference between a Fixed List and a Variable List is that the user can enter his or her own values in the field when the Type is a Variable List. For a Fixed List, the user can only choose one of the values in the list.

3.

Click on OK to complete the definition of the new custom property. Click on the down arrow to the right of the CPU field in the Custom Properties dialog box. The list of values you just defined are displayed; you can either choose one or enter another value.

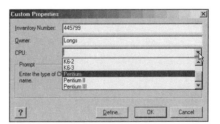

Reporting On Custom Properties

Often you will include important information in the Custom Properties for shapes. To retrieve this information, you would normally have to view the custom properties for each shape. However, Visio provides a better way: the Property Report.

1.

To create the Property Report, select Tools|Property Report to start the Property Reporting Wizard.

Click on the Next button.

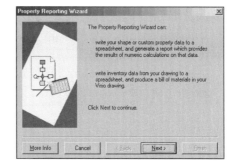

2.

To choose the specific shapes yourself, select Shapes You Select Yourself. Then, click on the Next button.

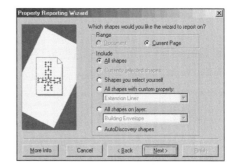

3.

On this panel, enter the name of the layer that will contain the shapes you are reporting on.

Click on Next.

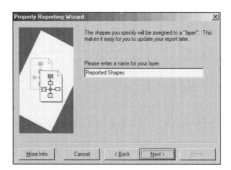

4.

This panel instructs you to choose the shapes you want to include. Do so by clicking on the first shape, then Shift-click to select multiple shapes.

Click on Next.

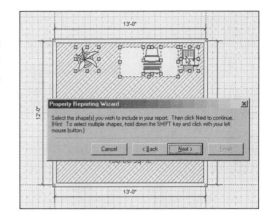

5.

Choose the properties you want to include in the report from the Properties column, and click on the arrow button to move the property to the Include column.

Click on Next.

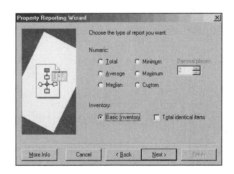

6.

On this panel, choose the type of report you want. For most cases, select Basic Inventory to get a listing of the items you specified.

Click on Next.

If you choose a Numeric report and any of the columns are not numeric, the resulting report will be blank. It is best to reserve numeric reports for custom properties, such as Cost.

7.

On this panel, choose the title for your report and the drawing page on which the report object should appear.

Click on Next.

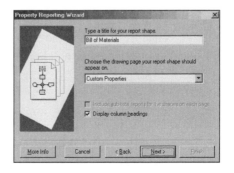

8.

On this panel, select the items you want to include on the report.

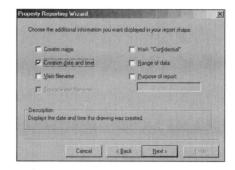

9.

Click on Next, and then click on Finish. The Property report appears on the page.

Working With Styles

With Visio 2000, you can predefine *styles*—combinations of text, line, and fill formatting. Applying a style to an object instantly changes the formatting of that object. This can be a great time-saver because you can apply the style to many objects to make their appearance consistent with each other. When changing a style, all the shapes that use that style will also change to match.

Applying Styles

The following steps will help you practice applying styles.

1.

Create a new drawing using the Basic Flowchart template (File|New|Flowchart|Basic Flowchart). Drag a process onto the empty drawing and type in "Text in a Rectangular Shape" to label the process. The default style for the shape is called Flow Normal and is visible in the Style drop-down menu at the left end of the toolbar.

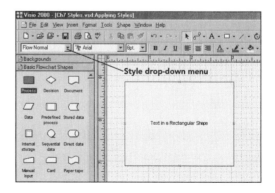

2.

The easiest way to apply a predefined style to a shape is to select the shape and choose the style from the Style drop-down menu.

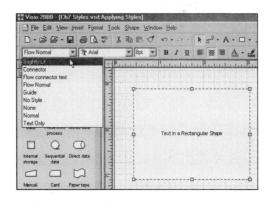

3.

This action applies all the elements of the pre-defined style: text, line, and fill.

The Brightly Lit and Darkness styles are not included in Visio 2000's default styles; you'll learn how to build these styles in the next section.

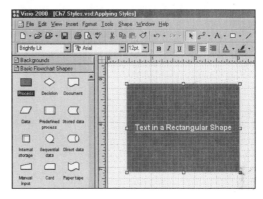

4.

You can also apply the individual elements of a style to an object. To do so, highlight the object and select Format|Style from either the main menu or the shortcut menu.

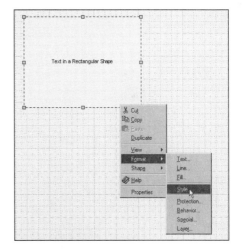

5.

This action opens the Style dialog box.

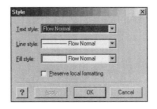

6.

To apply one of the Text styles, choose the text style you want from the Text Style drop-down menu.

Click on the Apply button to apply just the new Text Style to the shape.

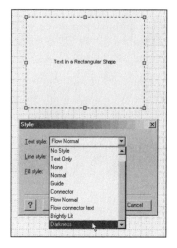

7.

To apply a Line style, choose the style you want from the Line Style drop-down menu.

Click on the Apply button to apply the new Line Style to the shape.

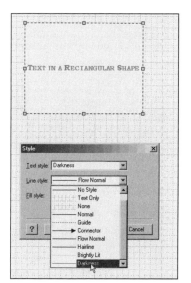

8.

Finally, to apply a Fill style, choose the style you want from the Fill Style drop-down menu.

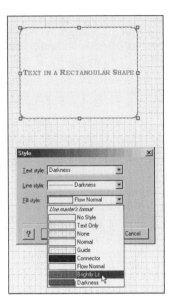

9.

Click on the Apply button to apply the new Fill style to the shape.

By using the Format|Style command, you can mix and match the Line, Fill, and Text styles. For example, you may want to apply a certain Text style to all shapes that represent a certain type of function performed by a given business organization.

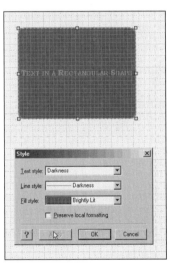

Editing And Creating Styles

You can define your own styles in Visio 2000. These styles are then available from the Style drop-down menu on the toolbar or from the Style dialog box.

1.

To define a new style, select Format|Define Styles from the main menu.

You can use all the techniques described in this section to modify an existing style as well. Just choose the style you want to modify from the Style drop-down menu, modify the style, and click on the Change button (which appears instead of the Add button when you are modifying an existing style).

2.

Type the name for the new style into the Style field. If you want to base the style on another, already-defined style, choose the style from the Based On drop-down menu.

3.

A style that you define does not *have* to define all three format types: Text, Line, and Fill. Clear the checkbox in the Includes section to disable any of the three format types in this style.

4.

To format the text properties for the Style, click on the Text button. This opens the Text dialog box. All the text formatting options discussed in Chapter 6 are available for formatting text in a particular style.

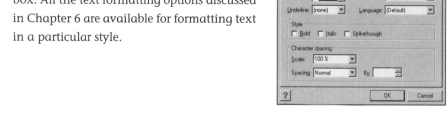

5.

To format the line properties for the Style, click on the Line button. This opens the Line dialog box. All the line formatting options discussed in Chapter 5 are available for formatting line in a style.

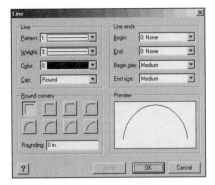

6.

To format the fill properties for the Style, click on the Fill button. This opens the Fill dialog box. All the fill formatting options discussed in Chapter 5 are available for formatting fill in a style.

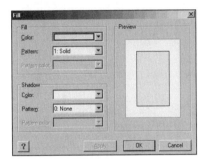

7.

After defining the style, click on the Add button to add it to the available styles. Then click on OK to close the dialog box.

8.

To apply the new style, select an object and choose the style from the Style drop-down menu on the toolbar.

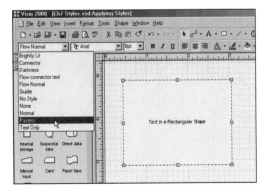

9.

The shape changes to use the new style.

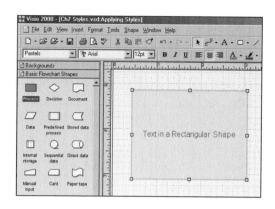

Numbering Shapes

It can be helpful to number the shapes in a diagram. You can choose to have Visio 2000 apply numbers when you create a shape or apply numbers to existing shapes on a page.

Certain special Visio 2000 solutions (such as Office Layout) do not allow shape numbering; the option for numbering is missing from the Tools menu.

1.

To number shapes, select Tools|Number Shapes to open the Number Shapes dialog box.

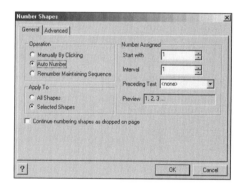

2.

The Auto Number option numbers either all the shapes on the page or just the selected shapes, depending on which option you have selected in the Apply To section of the dialog box.

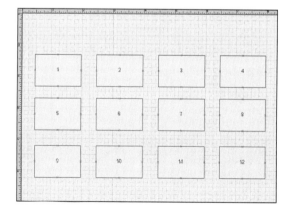

3.

If you select the Continue Numbering Shapes As Dropped On Page checkbox, then shapes you add to the page are numbered for you automatically.

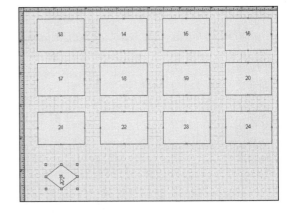

4.

The Number Assigned section enables you to set the starting number, the interval between numbers, and the text that precedes the number. Select the preceding text from the Preceding Text drop-down menu or type in the value you want.

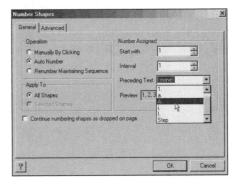

5.

The Preview field shows what the numbers will look like in the shapes.

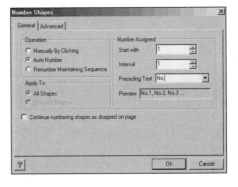

6.

In the Operation section of the dialog box, you can choose to number the shapes manually by clicking on them.

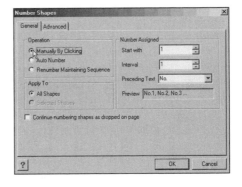

7.

Once you click on OK, the Manual Numbering dialog box opens on top of your drawing.

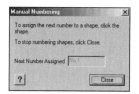

8.

Click on each shape you want to number. As you do, Visio 2000 adds the number to the shape.

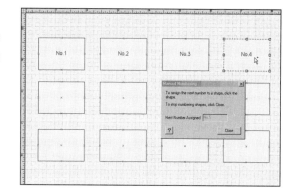

9.

When you have finished adding numbers, click on Close in the Manual Numbering dialog box.

Later, if you make changes to the drawing and the original numbering doesn't make sense, you can renumber the shapes. For example, take a look at this graphic. Notice how the shapes are no longer in the right order and that unnumbered shapes have been added.

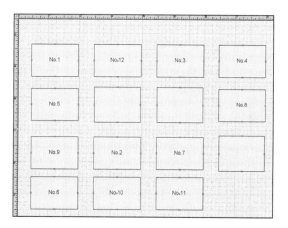

10.

To fix this situation, select Tools|Number Shapes and choose Renumber Maintaining Sequence from the Operation section. Reset the Start With field to 1 and click on OK. This renumbers the shapes and puts everything back in order.

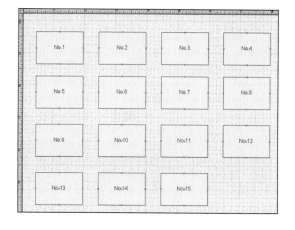

Using the Auto Number option can also renumber the shapes, but the order of the original numbering remains the same. For example, shape 12 remains 12, even though it was in the "No. 2" position. The new shapes receive numbers, but the Auto Number option doesn't change the numbering order of the existing shapes.

11.

The Advanced tab of the Number Shapes dialog box enables you to further configure how Visio 2000 numbers shapes.

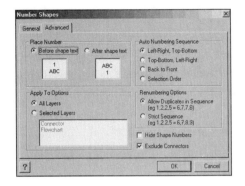

12.

In the Place Number section, you can decide whether the number is placed before or after existing text in the shape. For example, if you choose the After Shape Text radio button, the numbers are placed after the existing shape's text.

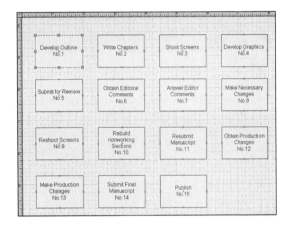

13.

You can change the sequence in which the numbers are applied. If you choose the Top-Bottom, Left-Right radio button, the numbering sequence is different from the previous example, which used Left-Right, Top-Bottom.

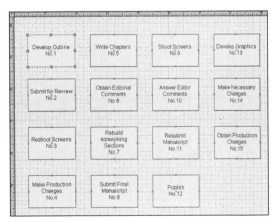

14.

You can also number the shapes in the order in which you selected them prior to choosing Tools|Number Shapes. To do this, click on the shape that you want to have the lowest number in the sequence. Then, Shift-click on the other shapes in the order that you want them numbered.

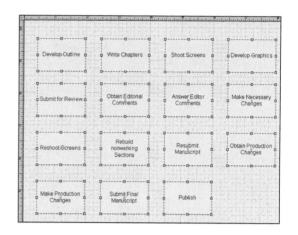

15.

Choose Selection Order in the Auto Numbering Sequence section of the Advanced tab and click on OK. The shapes are numbered in the order you selected them.

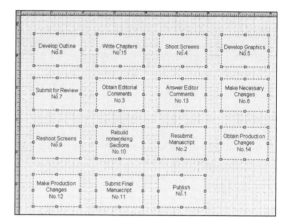

16.

The Renumbering Options section determines how shapes that are already numbered will be renumbered if there are duplicate numbers in the sequence. For example, if you choose the Allow Duplicates In Sequence option, two shapes that have the same number will continue to have the same number after renumbering. Here are the shapes before renumbering.

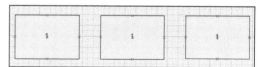

17.

And here is the screen after using Renumber Maintaining Sequence in the Number Shapes dialog box with a starting number of 2.

18.

If, instead, you choose the Strict Sequence option in the Renumbering Options section on the Advanced tab, the following graphic shows the same set of shapes after using Renumber Maintaining Sequence.

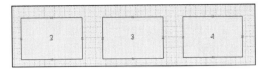

19.

You can also create a layer (see Chapter 9 for more information on creating layers and assigning shapes to them), assign shapes to that layer, and choose to number only the shapes on that layer. In this graphic, the shapes with heavy borders have been assigned to a layer called Numbered Shapes.

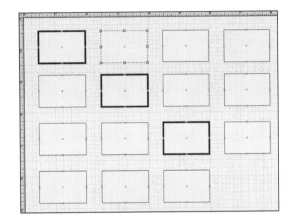

20.

From the Advanced tab of the Number Shapes dialog box, choose the Selected Layers option in the Apply To Options section.

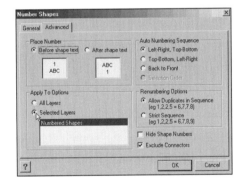

21.

Click on OK to number the shapes. Only those shapes assigned to this layer receive a number.

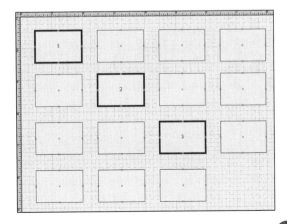

Creating Shapes Using Operations

Visio 2000 provides a huge number of shapes, but it may not provide a special shape that you need. However, all is not lost—you can create your own shapes by combining existing Visio shapes and performing a set of operations provided for just that purpose. This section teaches you how to create your own shapes, which you can save on your own stencils (see Chapter 8 for more information on creating stencils).

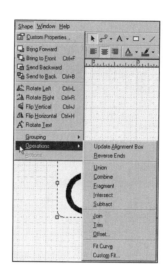

To use the various operations discussed in the next few sections, highlight the shapes to which you want to apply the operation, select Shape|Operations from the main menu, and choose the operation you want to use.

Using The Union Operation

This graphic shows three shapes. The two lower crosses overlap.

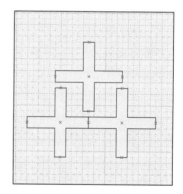

Shape|Operations|Union
After the Union operation, the three shapes become one and any overlaps merge.

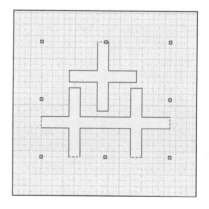

Using The Fragment Operation

In this graphic, I performed the Fragment operation on the shape that resulted from the previous Union operation. Any non-overlapping shapes revert back to their original shapes using this operation—effectively undoing the Union operation for those shapes.

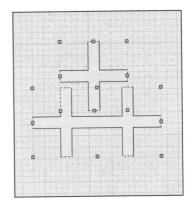

Using The Combine Operation

To experiment with the Combine operation, I'll start with four overlapping crosses and two overlapping rectangles.

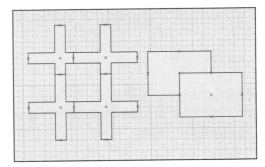

Shape|Operations|Combine

When you use the Combine operation on the overlapping crosses, it joins them to produce one shape, but any overlapping sections are left *out* of the resulting shape. This is easier to see with the overlapping rectangles.

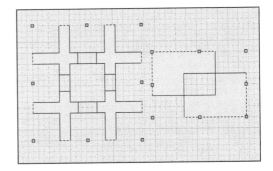

Using The Intersect Operation

To experiment with the Intersect operation, I'll use two overlapping arrows.

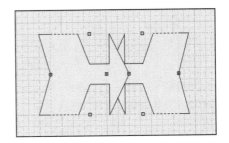

Shape|Operations|Intersect

When you use the Intersect operation, Visio forms a new shape from just those areas where *all* the included shapes overlap.

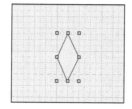

Using The Subtract Operation

To experiment with the Subtract operation, I'll use a shadowed box and a partially overlapping arrow.

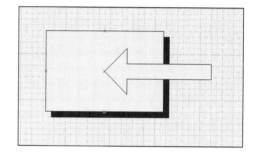

Shape|Operations|Subtract

When you apply the Subtract operation, Visio subtracts the second (and subsequent) shape(s) from the first shape to create the result. In this example, I selected the shadowed box first, then the arrow. As a result, the arrow was subtracted from the box.

Using The Join Operation

To experiment with the Join operation, I'll use an overlapping rectangle and an oval.

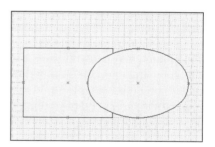

Shape|Operations|Join

When you apply the Join operation, Visio creates a new shape that includes *only* the outlines of the selected shapes as shown in this graphic. The grid shows through where the white interior of the shapes used to be.

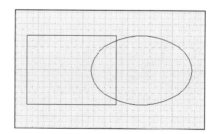

Using The Trim Operation

To experiment with the Trim operation, I'll use an overlapping cross and rectangle.

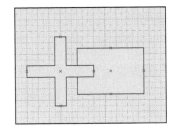

Shape|Operations|Trim

When you apply the Trim operation, all line segments are converted to independent "shapes," which you can move around. You can see from the graphic that individual line segments are selected. How is this useful? You got me!

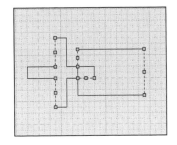

Using The Offset Operation

To demonstrate the Offset operation, I'll use a pair of touching crosses.

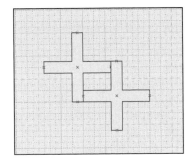

Shape|Operations|Offset

When you apply the Offset operation, you can specify an offset distance. Once you do, the selected shapes are redrawn with their borders offset by the specified amount. In this graphic, an offset of 0.25 inches was specified for both crosses.

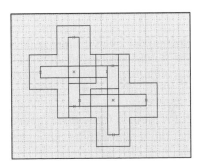

Using Fit Curve

To demonstrate the Trim operation, I'll use several angular shapes, including a cross, a square, an arrow, and a triangle.

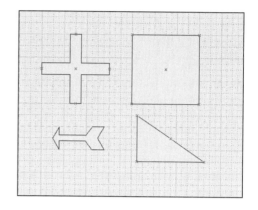

Shape|Operations|Fit Curve

The Fit Curve operation converts all the shapes to smooth curves—giving an interesting (and somewhat puzzling) effect.

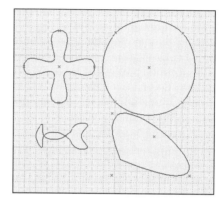

Modifying Shape Behavior

You can customize how a shape behaves within a group, how it interacts with other shapes, which parts of the shape are visible, and how the shape responds when you double-click on it. This section shows you how to customize shape behaviors.

1.

To change the behavior of a shape or a group, right-click on the shape or group and select Format|Behavior from the shortcut menu.

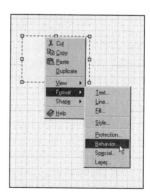

2.

This opens the Behavior dialog box for a shape. The Behavior dialog box for a group has more options—I'll look at it shortly.

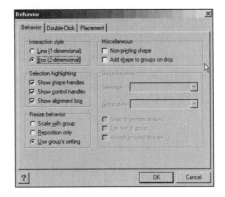

3.

The Selection Highlighting section of the dialog box controls which items appear when you select a shape. For example, if you turn off all of these items by clearing their checkboxes, a shape looks exactly the same whether it is selected or not. In this graphic, only the Shape Handles are turned on.

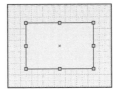

4.

The Resize Behavior controls how an object resizes when it is part of a group. For example, let's use the cross that is grouped with the rectangle in this graphic.

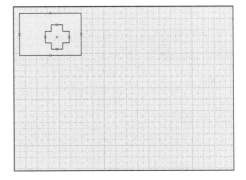

5.

If the Resize Behavior is set to Scale With Group, then dragging the group to resize it resizes the included shape as well.

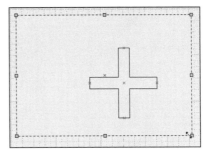

6.

On the other hand, if the Reposition Only option is selected, then the included shape does *not* change size; it merely moves as much as needed to remain in the same relative position inside the group.

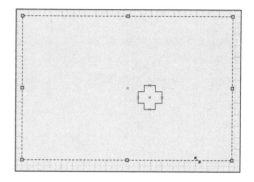

7.

The Miscellaneous section enables you to tag an object as non-printing. It also enables you to specify that if you drag an object onto a group, Visio will add it to the group automatically, provided the group's behavior allows this (more on this momentarily). When you drag a shape with the Add Shape To Groups On Drop checkbox selected, the edge of the group is shaded to indicate that the shape will be accepted.

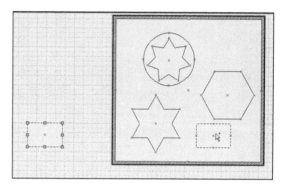

The Accept Dropped Shapes checkbox must be selected in the Group Behavior section of the Behavior dialog box for a group in order for the dropped shape to be accepted by the group.

8.

The group version of the Behavior dialog box has many more available options in the Group Behavior section.

9.

The Selection drop-down menu specifies what happens when you click on a group. Group First specifies that the first time you click on a shape in a group, the group is selected.

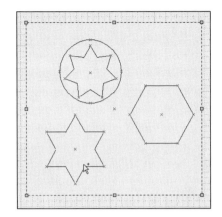

10.

The second time you click on a shape in a group, the shape is selected.

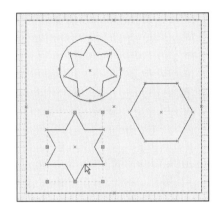

11.

If you choose Group Only, you can only click on the group. If you choose Members First, clicking on a shape in a group selects that shape rather than the group.

The Snap To Member Shapes checkbox determines whether a connector can connect only to the perimeter of the group (when the checkbox is off)…

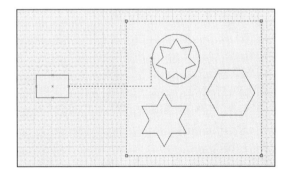

12.

or to the connection handles on the included shapes (when the checkbox is on).

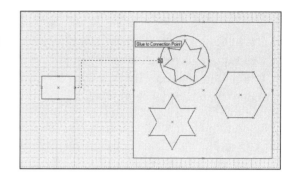

13.

The Edit Text Of Group checkbox enables you to attach text to the group—just as you can attach text to a shape.

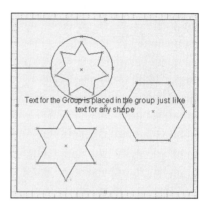

14.

The Group Data drop-down menu determines how the group's text will appear. If you choose the setting In Front Of Member Shapes, the result will be much like the previous graphic. However, if you choose the setting Behind Member Shapes, any part of the text that coincides with a shape in the group is hidden.

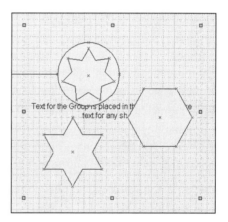

Setting Shape Double-Click Action

A Visio 2000 shape can respond in a variety of ways when you double-click on it. In this section, you will learn how to change the action that Visio takes when you double-click on a shape.

1.

To change the shape's double-click behavior, choose the Double-Click tab on the Behavior dialog box.

Each type of shape has a default action defined for it. For most shapes, this action edits the shape's text, but some shapes have a different default action. Choosing the option Perform Default Action completes whatever default action is defined for that shape. Because the default actions aren't documented anywhere, this function isn't particularly useful!

2.

If you choose the Perform No Action option, nothing happens when you double-click on the shape. If you choose Edit Shape's Text, double-clicking on the shape puts you in text-edit mode, where you can edit and format the shape's text.

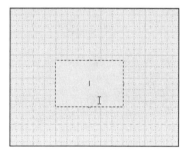

3.

If you choose the Open Shape's ShapeSheet
option, a special spreadsheet opens that defines all the attributes of the shape. This
shapesheet is extremely complex and most
people don't use it.

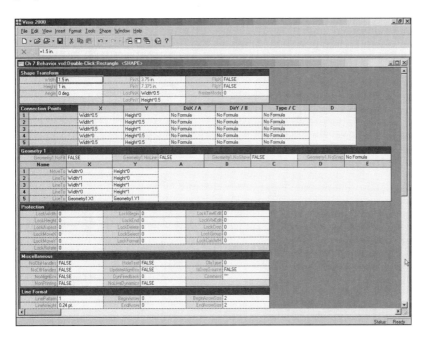

4.

If you choose the Run Macro option, you can
run any macro by simply double-clicking on
the shape. For example, let's say you selected
the Custom Properties Editor from the drop-
down menu.

5.

Double-clicking on the shape launches the Custom Properties Editor.

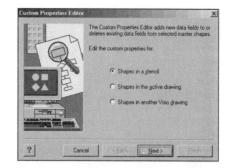

6.

You can also use a shape to jump to another page in the document. Choose the Go To Page option, and choose the page you want to jump to from the drop-down menu.

7.

If you want the page to open in a new
window, select the Open In New Window
checkbox. Double-clicking on the shape opens
a new window displaying the selected page.

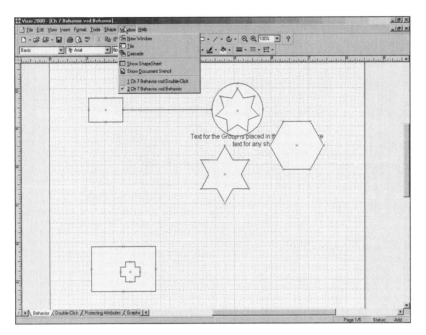

Protecting Shape Attributes

You can protect aspects of shapes so that the casual user can't change them. This can be important when you have gone to a lot of work to set up a shape and you don't want to allow
modifications to the attributes of that shape.

1.

To protect shape attributes, select
Format|Protection from the shortcut menu or
main menu. This displays the Protection dialog box.

2.

If you select the Width box, small "locks" appear on the left and right edges of the shape indicating that the width cannot be changed. The Height protection works in the same way.

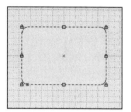

If you try to change the width by dragging a locked sizing handle with the mouse, nothing happens. If you try to change the width from the Size and Position window, you can change the width setting, but it changes back the moment you leave the Width field.

3.

Protecting the Aspect ratio maintains the height/width ratio—dragging any sizing handle resizes the entire shape to maintain the ratio. For example, if you drag a width sizing handle, it resizes both the width and the height.

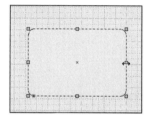

4.

The Begin Point checkbox has no effect on closed shapes, but it keeps you from moving the beginning point of a connector. The End Point checkbox works in the same way.

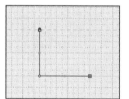

Selecting the X Position box makes it impossible to drag the shape left and right; selecting the Y Position box makes it impossible to drag the shape up and down.

5.

Selecting the Rotation checkbox stops the shape from being rotated by placing small locks at the rotation handles and the center of rotation.

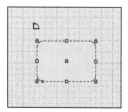

6.

If you select the From Deletion box, you won't be able to delete the shape. If you try (for example, by pressing the Delete key), Visio warns you that you can't delete the shape.

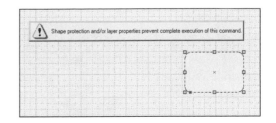

7.

Finally, if you select the From Selection box, Visio warns you that you can still select the shape unless you enable shape protection.

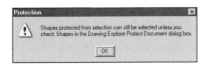

Enabling Shape Protection

To enable shape protection, do the following:

1.

Select View|Windows|Drawing Explorer from the main menu. This opens the Drawing Explorer Window.

2.

Right-click on the file name displayed at the top of the window, and select Protect Document from the shortcut menu.

3.

In the Protect Document dialog box, select the Shapes checkbox. Then, select OK to enable Shape protection.

Working With Graphics And Clip Art

Visio 2000 enables you to work with graphics and clip art by providing most of the same operations used with Visio shapes. For example, you can join two pieces of clip art using a connector. This section shows you how to add graphics and clip art to a Visio drawing and how to modify the graphics once you've got them in your drawing.

Adding A Graphic To A Visio Drawing

In this section you'll practice adding a graphic to a Visio drawing.

1.

Select Insert|Picture from the menu. This displays the Picture menu for you to choose a picture file.

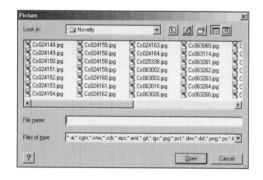

2.

Visio can open a huge variety of graphic files including all the Internet-format files. To choose a specific type of file, select the type from the Files Of Type drop-down menu.

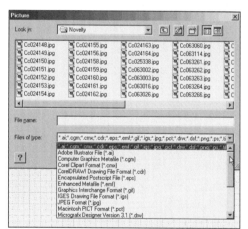

3.

Select a file and click on the Open button. This places the graphic on the Visio drawing.

Adding Clip Art To A Visio Drawing

In this section you'll add clip art to a Visio drawing.

1.

Select Insert|Clip Art from the menu. If you have the Microsoft Clip Gallery installed (it comes with many Microsoft products, including Office), you'll see the Microsoft Clip Gallery dialog box.

2.

Choose a piece of clip art from the collection and click on the Insert button. This places the clip art in the diagram.

Some types of graphic files (including both gifs and jpegs) require additional parameters in order to be imported properly. In these cases, Visio provides the appropriate dialog box so you can input the parameters.

Modifying The Graphics And Clip Art

Much of what you can do with "regular" Visio shapes you can do with graphics and clip art. For example, you can click on the clip art and resize it to make it smaller.

1.

You can click and drag a graphic or clip art to move it on the page.

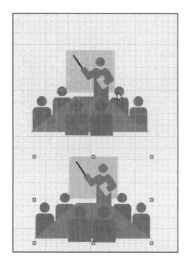

2.

You can also add custom properties by selecting View|Custom Properties from the shortcut menu. Of course, a graphic or clip art doesn't have custom properties initially, but you can define them from the Custom Properties window if you wish.

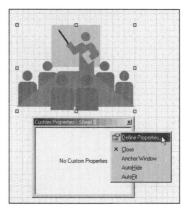

3.

As with other Visio shapes, you can connect clip art and graphics using connectors.

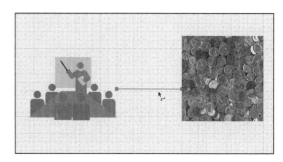

4.

You can also add text and format the text by selecting Format|Text from the shortcut menu.

5.

You can apply fill and line formatting to clip art and graphics as well—even a shadow. Just use the Format|Fill and Format|Line selections from the shortcut menu—like a regular Visio shape.

6.

You can rotate a shape using the Rotation tool. Just choose the Rotation tool, and click on one of the rotation handles for the graphic.

7.

Then drag the graphic to its new rotation angle.

8.

Finally, using the shortcut menu, you can stack, group, and rotate/flip the graphic.

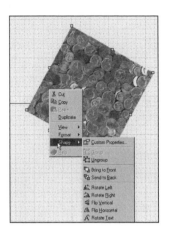

Adding Hyperlinks To Shapes

Earlier, I mentioned that you can configure a shape to jump to another page in a drawing when you double-click on it. But, Visio 2000's shapes are much more versatile than that. You can use Visio 2000's shapes as hyperlinks to link to other Visio files, URLs on the Internet, or even a file from a different application altogether. In fact, you can attach multiple hyperlinks to a shape and mix and match the types.

Adding The Background

To demonstrate the power of hyperlinks, I'm going to create a set of "buttons" that enable hyperlinks. To follow along, create a new drawing by selecting File|New|Block Diagram|Basic Diagram. Switch to the Backgrounds stencil and drag the Background Cosmic shape onto the page. Answer "yes" when it asks you to confirm that you want to use this shape as the background. This step isn't really necessary, but it will make the final result look better.

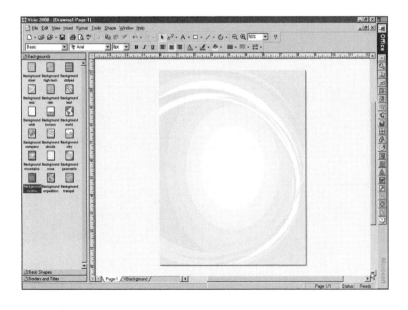

Creating The Buttons

Zoom the page to 100% and drag four Shadowed boxes from the Basic Shapes stencil. Line them up at the top of the drawing and label them "Visio Drawing", "Word Document", "Internet", and "Multiple". Select all four boxes and change the text size to 12 pt. (use the drop-down menu on the toolbar).

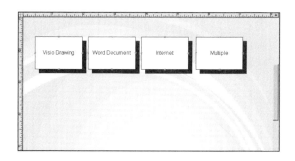

If you don't have Microsoft Word, you can still follow along, you'll just have to open a file for an application you do have. Just label the second box with the name of the application you will be using (for example, "WordPerfect Document", "Paint Shop Pro Document", and so on).

Building A Visio Drawing Hyperlink

To use Visio 2000's shapes as hyperlinks to link to other Visio files, follow along with these steps.

1.

Highlight the first box labeled Visio Drawing, and select Insert|Hyperlinks from the main menu.

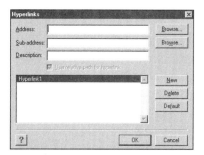

2.

Click on the Browse button alongside the Address field in the Hyperlinks dialog box. Choose Local File from the drop-down menu that appears.

3.

From the Link To File dialog box, choose a Visio file to link to.

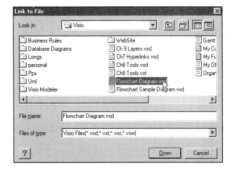

4.

Click on Open to return to the Hyperlinks dialog box. If the Visio drawing you are selecting has more than one page, and you want to jump immediately to a page that is not the first page in the drawing, click on the Browse button alongside the Sub-Address field. This opens an additional Hyperlink dialog box.

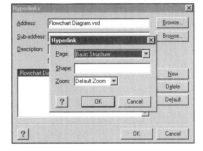

5.

Click on the Page drop-down menu, and choose the page in the target diagram that you want to be visible when you trigger the hyperlink. You may also choose the zoom level from the Zoom drop-down menu.

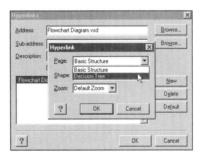

6.

Click on OK to return to the main Hyperlinks dialog box. Click on OK again to close the Hyperlinks dialog box. Move the mouse cursor over the Visio Drawing box. Notice how the cursor turns into the classic Hyperlink symbol. This indicates that a hyperlink is available from that shape. If you hover the mouse over the shape, a tool tip pops up to tell you the hyperlink destination.

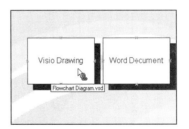

7.

Now, let's trigger the hyperlink. To do so, right-click on the shape. The hyperlink appears in the shortcut menu.

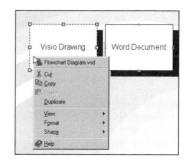

8.

Choose the hyperlink from the shortcut menu and the Visio diagram opens to the page you selected when you defined the hyperlink.

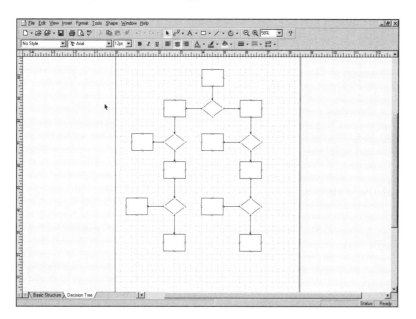

Building A Word Document Hyperlink

Now, you'll use a Visio 2000 shape to hyperlink to a Word document.

1.

To build a Word document hyperlink, select the Word Document box (or whatever box you created), and then select Insert|Hyperlinks from the main menu. Click on the Browse button alongside the Address field in the Hyperlinks dialog box, and choose Local File from the drop-down menu that appears. In the Link To File dialog box, choose All Files from the Files Of Type drop-down menu.

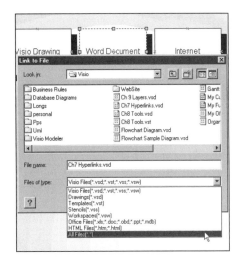

2.

Navigate to a directory that contains Word documents (*.doc), and choose a document to link to.

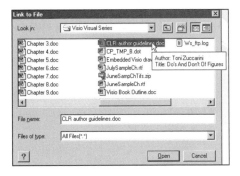

3.

Click on OK to return to the Hyperlinks dialog box.

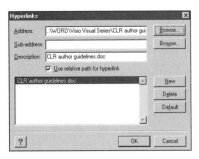

4.

Click on OK to close the Hyperlinks Dialog box.

To activate the hyperlink, right-click on the Word Document box, and choose the hyperlink from the shortcut menu.

5.

Word (or your application) opens and loads the document you chose.

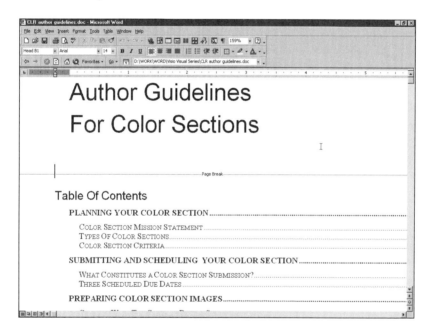

Building An Internet Hyperlink

Internet hyperlinks are very useful. Using this Visio feature, you can create a set of "buttons" that connect to your favorite sites on the Internet.

1.

To build an Internet hyperlink, highlight the Internet box and select Insert|Hyperlinks from the main menu. Click on the Browse button alongside the Address field in the Hyperlinks dialog box, and choose Internet Address from the drop-down menu that appears.

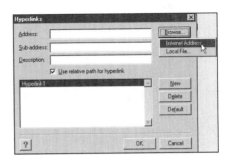

For the rest of this exercise to work, you must have a live connection to the Internet.

2.

At this point, your default browser launches, and you are connected to Visio's Web site.

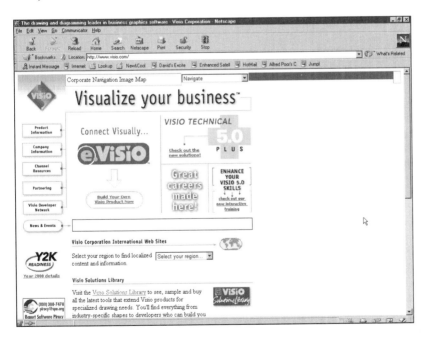

3.

Navigate to the Web site to which you want to link, using your standard browser controls. In this case, we used the Coriolis home page, **www.coriolis.com**, as our target.

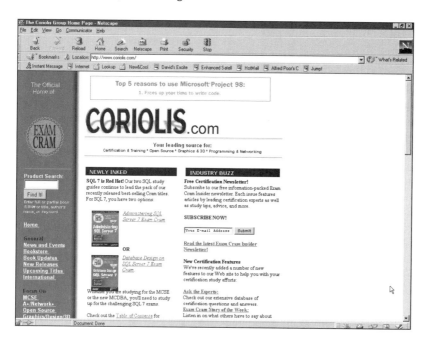

4.

Switch back to Visio, and notice that the Web address to which you navigated is now in the Address field of the Hyperlinks dialog box. Click on OK to close the Hyperlinks dialog box.

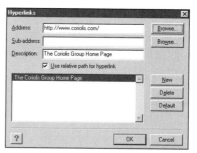

5.

To activate the hyperlink, right-click on the Internet box, and choose the hyperlink from the shortcut menu. Your browser will open (if it's not open already) and navigate to the Internet site chosen.

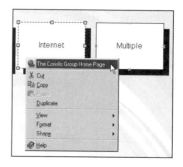

Building Multiple Hyperlinks

In the final section of this chapter, you'll attach multiple hyperlinks to a shape.

1.

Highlight the Multiple box and select Insert|Hyperlinks from the main menu. Click on the Browse button alongside the Address field in the Hyperlinks dialog box, and choose Local File from the drop-down menu that appears. From the Link To File dialog box, choose the file type from the Files Of Type drop-down menu, and select the file.

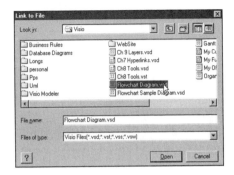

2.

Click on Open to add the hyperlink to the Hyperlinks dialog box. Then, click on the New button to add another hyperlink.

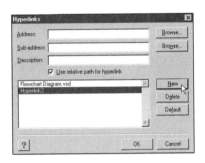

3.

Type **http://www.visio.com** into the Address field. Add a description, such as "A great drawing tool company", in the Description field. Press the tab key, and your changes are added to the new hyperlink.

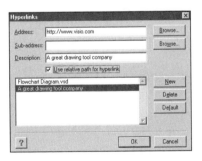

4.

Click on the New button *again* to add another
new hyperlink. Type **http://www.coriolis.com**
in the Address field and "Books and More from
Coriolis" in the Description field.

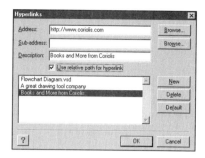

5.

Click on OK to finish adding hyperlinks. Now,
right-click on the Multiple box. The three
hyperlinks you created are visible at the top
of the shortcut menu; simply choose one to
activate that hyperlink.

Chapter 8
Creating Your Own
Visio Tools

- Create a new stencil for holding existing shapes and new shapes

- Create a new master shape for a stencil, including setting the properties and specifying how the shape's stencil icon appears

- Create a new template that groups your own set of stencils

Creating Stencils, Shapes, And Templates

Visio 2000 comes with a wide variety of stencils that contain a huge number of shapes. However, if you don't find exactly what you need on a stencil, you can create your own stencils, populate them with new *master* shapes, and even group a set of stencils into your own template. This chapter shows you how to create a stencil, a master shape, specify the properties of stencils and master shapes, and create your own templates.

Creating New Stencils

Stencils are the palettes of shapes that you use as a source for placing shapes on a drawing. Visio comes with a large variety of stencils, which may be all you'll ever need. However, you may wish to create your own stencils so that you can group the shapes you use most or use them as a "home" for the master shapes that you build yourself.

1.

First, select File|New|Blank Drawing to create a new drawing without stencils. To create a new stencil, select File|Stencils|New Stencil.

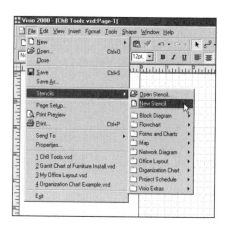

2.

Visio 2000 creates a new, blank stencil with a default name.

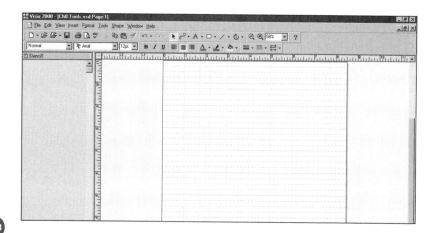

3.

To name and save the stencil, click on the icon in the upper-left corner of the stencil and choose Save.

4.

Enter a name for the stencil, such as "My Custom Stencil", and click on the Save button. This displays the Properties dialog box, where you can enter the Subject, Author, and other information.

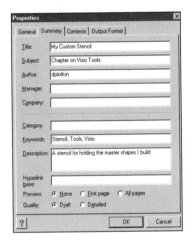

5.

Click on OK to save these changes to your stencil.

6.

You can make the stencil editable by clicking on the icon in the upper-left corner of the stencil to display the menu and choose Edit from the menu. The Edit selection is a toggle—select it again to turn off the ability to edit the stencil. You can edit the shapes on the stencil, add and remove shapes, and change the stencil properties.

Creating New Master Shapes

Master shapes are the shapes that appear on a stencil. In this section, you are going to learn how to build your own master shapes.

Creating A Master From A Visio Shape

If you have built a normal Visio shape, you can create a master shape from it. For example, this graphic shows a set of shapes selected from the Basic Flowchart Shapes stencil and grouped together into a single shape.

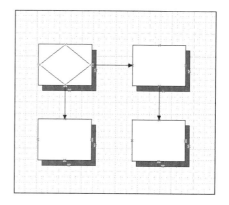

1.

To add this shape to your stencil, click and drag the shape onto the stencil.

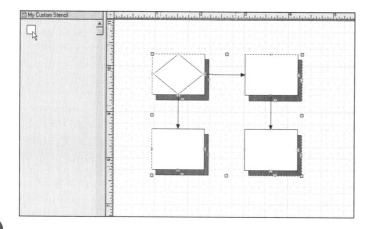

2.

Visio adds the shape to the stencil and creates a default icon for the shape.

When you drag the shape from the drawing area to the stencil, the shape is moved to the stencil; it is no longer in the drawing area. If you want to retain the shape in the drawing area and add it to the stencil, press the Ctrl key before dragging the shape. This action copies the shape to the stencil. Also, notice the disk icon that appears in the upper-right corner of the stencil. This indicates that a change has been made to the stencil and requires you to save the stencil. To save the stencil, click on the disk icon.

3.

You can change the name of the shape by clicking on the shape, pausing, and clicking on the shape again. This highlights the name so you can enter a new name, such as "Four Boxes".

4.

To change the properties of the master shape, right-click on the shape and choose Master Properties from the shortcut menu.

5.

This opens the Master Properties dialog box.

6.

From this dialog box, you can change the name, choose the alignment of the name on the icon, and choose the size of the icon from the Icon Size drop-down menu.

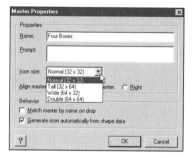

7.

You can also use the Prompt field to specify the text that will appear when you hover the mouse over the shape.

8.

After filling in the prompt, click on OK. Then, hover the mouse over the master shape to see the prompt.

9.

The Generate Icon Automatically From Shape Data is selected by default; if you want to override the default icon with your own icon design, clear this checkbox.

You can change the master shape by either double-clicking on the shape in the stencil or by choosing Edit Master from the shape's shortcut menu. This opens a window in which you can use the standard Visio tools to modify the master shape.

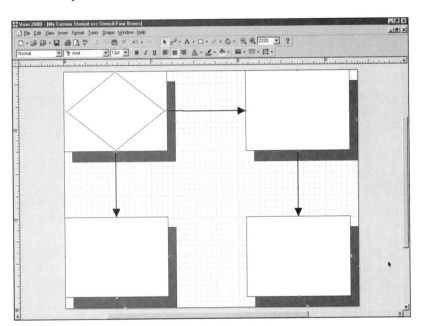

10.

Let's make some changes to the master shape. Add "Yes" and "No" text to the decision lines, add a title block in the middle, add a date, and add a fill color to the diamond shape.

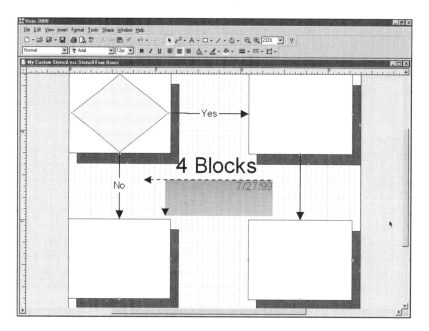

11.

Click on the close button in the upper-right corner of the window to close the window. Visio will query you as to whether you want to update the master shape.

12.

Click on Yes and the window closes, updating the shape in the stencil.

Creating A Master Shape From Scratch

Starting from scratch is another way to create a new master shape.

1.

Right-click in the stencil area, and choose New Master from the shortcut menu. The stencil must be editable for this to work.

2.

Fill out the properties of the new master shape in the New Master dialog box.

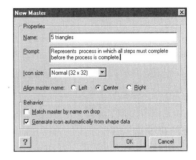

3.

Visio 2000 places the new shape in the stencil. However, because you haven't defined the shape yet, there is no icon (other than the default "X").

4.

Double-click on the new master shape to open the window to build the shape. Go ahead and build the shape.

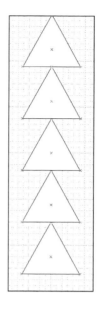

5.

Close the window (saving the results when queried), and place the new icon for the master shape in the stencil.

Creating A Master Shape From An Existing Master Shape

You can also create a new master shape based on an existing one.

1.

Open the appropriate stencil, and select the shape you want to add to your stencil. Right-click on the shape and choose Copy from the shortcut menu.

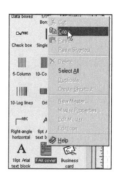

2.

Return to your stencil, right-click in an empty area, and choose Paste from the shortcut menu.

3.

The new shape appears in the stencil and can be modified as described in the previous sections.

Modifying The Master Shape Icon

As seen earlier, Visio 2000 provides a default icon for a master shape. However, if you wish, you can create your own icon.

1.

To do so, right-click on the master shape in the stencil, and choose Edit Icon from the shortcut menu.

2.

Visio 2000 displays the Icon editing tool in a new window. This tool has its own set of drawing tools.

1. Left Color

2. Right Color

3. Color palette

4. Transparent color

5. Pencil tool

6. Bucket (Fill) tool

7. Lasso

8. Selection Net tool

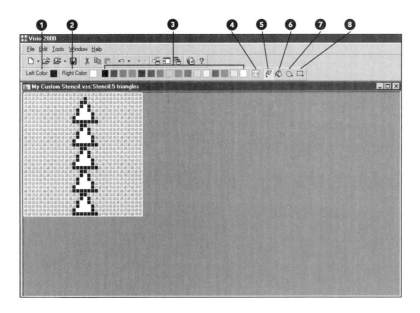

3.

The most common way to make changes to an icon is to use the Pencil tool. Click on the color you want to draw with using the left mouse button, then right-click on the color you want to draw with using the right mouse button. Begin making changes to the icon—one pixel at a time.

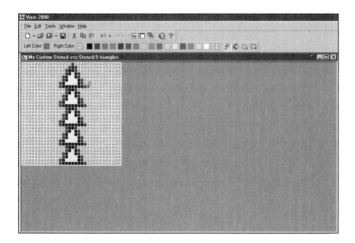

4.

When you're finished making changes to the icon, click on the close box in the upper-right corner of the window. The master shape icon reflects the changes to the stencil. Don't forget to save the stencil to preserve those changes.

Creating New Templates

A Visio 2000 template is a grouping of stencils and a drawing, which may have more than one page. Visio 2000 comes with many specialized templates; I have used the Basic Flowchart template quite a bit throughout this book. However, you can build your own, special-purpose templates. In this section, you will learn how to do this.

1.

To compose a template, open the stencils you want included in the template.

2.

Then, make any changes to the drawing page that you want to *always* appear when you open the template.

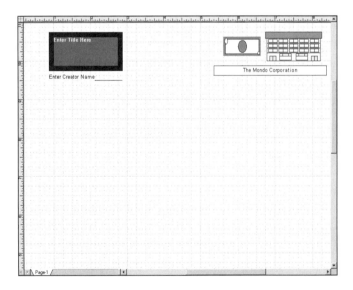

3.

Select File|Properties to open the Properties dialog box. In the description field, enter the description you want to appear when you click on this template. Click on OK.

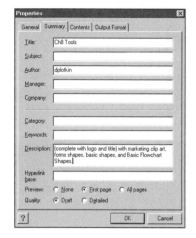

4.

Select File|Save As, and choose Template (*.vst) from the Save As Type drop-down menu on the Save As dialog box. Be sure to save the template in the directory designated for templates (by default, this is Visio 2000/Solutions). In this example, I created a folder inside the Solutions folder called "My Templates".

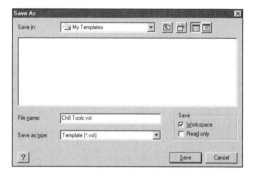

5.

To try out your new template, close the file. Then select File|New|My Templates and choose the name of the template you want to view (Ch8 Tools in this example).

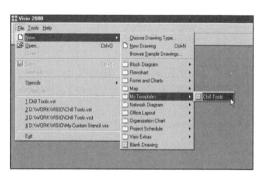

6.

Alternatively, you can select File|New|Choose Drawing Type, and click on the My Templates folder to display a preview of the template. Pause the mouse over the template to see the description for the template.

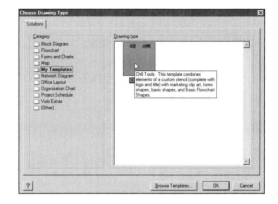

7.

Click on OK to open the template, which now consists of all the stencils and any prebuilt drawing pages. Look familiar?

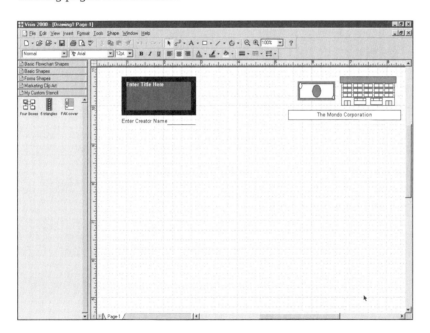

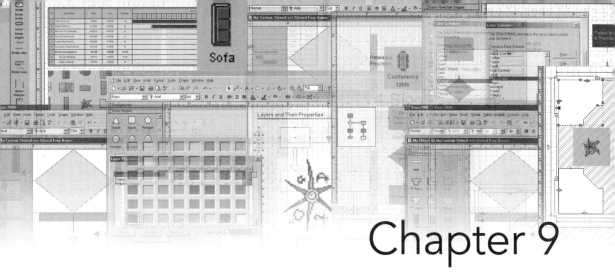

Chapter 9
Controlling Shapes
With Layers

- Learn what layers are and how they interact with a diagram

- Create and remove layers in a drawing

- Set layer properties

- Assign shapes to layers

Exercising Control

You can exercise control over sets of shapes that are assigned to layers in a diagram. You can set properties for a layer and apply sophisticated operations to shapes in a layer, such as running a Property Report on only the shapes in a certain layer. In this chapter, you will learn to create and delete layers, assign shapes to layers, and set layer properties.

Every drawing has at least two layers when you create it. The first layer (named for the drawing file) is the default layer on which all shapes are placed when you drag them onto the drawing. The other layer is the connector layer; all connectors you create are placed by default in this layer. These layers are not visible in the Layers dialog box, but they *are* visible when working with tools (such as the Property Report Wizard, see Chapter 7) that use layers.

Creating New Layers

To exercise control over the layers in a drawing, you must first create the layers you need.

1.

Create a new diagram by selecting File| New|Block Diagram|Basic Diagram from the main menu. To create a layer, select View|Layer Properties to open the Layer Properties dialog box.

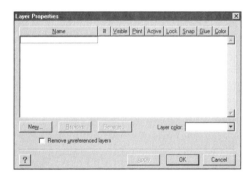

2.

Click on the New button to display the New Layer dialog box.

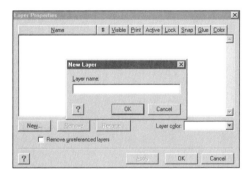

3.

Enter a name, such as "Printable Shapes", and click on the OK button to create the new layer. Visio 2000 sets the default properties for the new level, as indicated by the checkboxes.

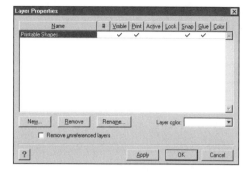

4.

Create another layer called "Unprintable Shapes".

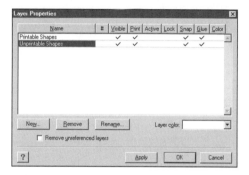

5.

Click under the Active heading for the Printable Shapes layer to make this the active layer—the layer on which new shapes will be added by default when you drag them onto the diagram.

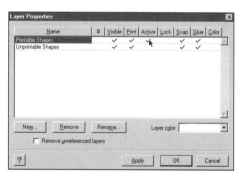

6.

Clear the checkmark under the Print heading for the Unprintable Shapes layer, because you don't want any shapes on that layer to print.

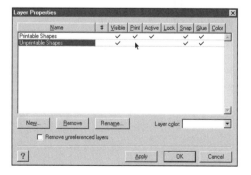

7.

Create another layer called "Overlay".

8.

Click on OK to close the Layer Properties dialog box.

Switch to the Borders and Titles stencil, and drag the Border Graduated shape onto the page. Double-click on the word Title and enter "Layers and Their Properties".

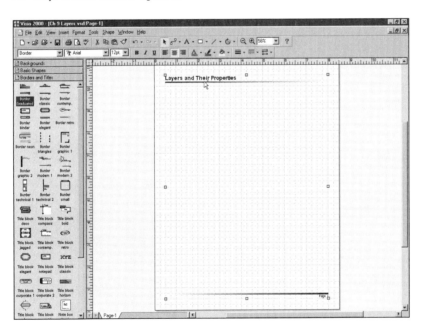

9.

Drag the Title Block Corporate 2 shape onto the page and place it in the lower-right corner. Double-click on the words Company Name and type "The Coriolis Effect".

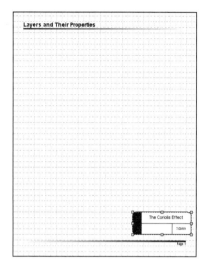

10.

Switch to the Basic Shapes template, and add the shapes shown in this graphic.

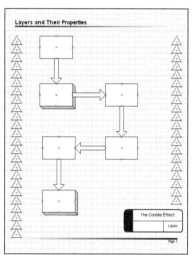

11.

Now reopen the Layer Properties dialog box (View|Layer Properties) and click on the # button. This updates the number of shapes in each layer. Notice that all the shapes appear in the Printable Shapes layer because you set it as the Active layer.

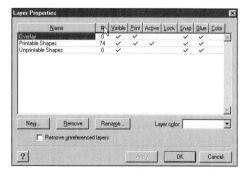

Assigning Shapes To Layers

As mentioned earlier, shapes are assigned by default to the Active layer. However, you can reassign shapes to different layers to take advantage of various layer properties. In this section, you are going to change the layer assignments of shapes and adjust the layer properties to get the effects you want.

1.

Select the Layers and Their Properties top/bottom border. Right-click on this object and choose Format|Layer from the shortcut menu. This opens the Layer dialog box. The selected layer is the one to which this shape is currently assigned.

2.

Choose Overlay from the list to change the layer assignment to the Overlay layer.

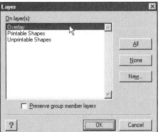

3.

Click on OK to close the dialog box. Now highlight all the triangles along the left edge of the page, and choose Format|Layer from the main menu. In the Layer dialog box, choose Unprintable Shapes.

4.

Click on OK to return to the drawing. Repeat this operation with the triangles along the right side of the page, and click on OK.

Select View|Layer Properties, and click on the # button to update the shape counts. Notice that each of the layers has shapes assigned to it.

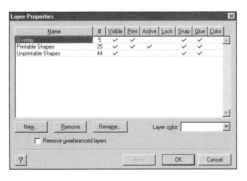

5.

Click under Lock for the Overlay layer. This locks the layer, preventing you from adding or removing shapes from the layer. You also cannot drag or resize the shapes. In fact, you can't select any shape in the layer at all.

Place a checkmark under Color for the Un-printable Shapes layer, and choose a bright green from the Layer Color drop-down menu.

A layer cannot be both locked and active at the same time.

6.

Click on OK and notice what happens to the triangles; they turn to the bright green chosen for the layer. This helps you identify which shapes are on which layer.

The color of the triangles' border lines is not green; it is still whatever color you set (or the default, if you didn't set a color). The layer color overrides all line colors.

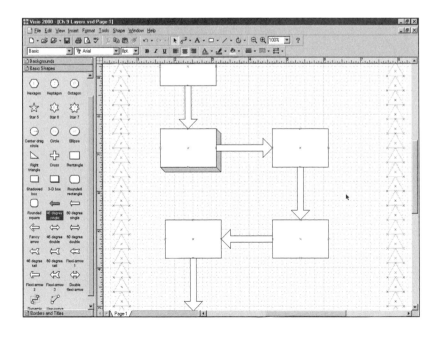

7.

Reopen the Layer Properties dialog box and clear the Visible property for the Overlay layer, click on OK, and take a look at the drawing—the top/bottom border has disappeared.

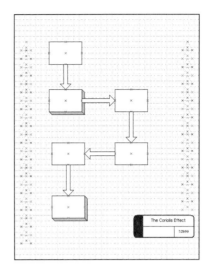

8.

Right-click on the title bar shape, and choose Format|Layer from the shortcut menu to open the Layer dialog box. Click on the Unprintable Shapes layer and click on OK to close the dialog box. The shape takes on the green color of the layer it was assigned to.

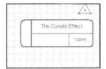

Did you wonder why the Overlay layer wasn't available in the Layer dialog box? It is because the layer is locked. You can't assign shapes to a locked layer.

9.

Let's rename the Unprintable Shapes layer to Nonprinting Shapes. Select View|Layer Properties to open the Layer Properties dialog box, select the Unprintable Shapes layer, and click on Rename.

10.

Enter "Nonprinting Shapes", and click on the OK button. Visio 2000 changes the name of the layer.

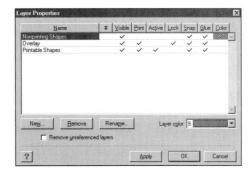

Deleting A Layer

You can delete a layer, but you need to be careful—all shapes on that layer are deleted along with the layer.

1.

To delete a layer, such as the Nonprinting Shapes layer, select View|Layer Properties to open the Layer Properties dialog box. Choose the Nonprinting Shapes layer, and click on Remove. Visio 2000 warns you that all shapes on the layer will be deleted and asks you to confirm the deletion.

2.

Click on Yes, and the Layer is removed from the dialog box.

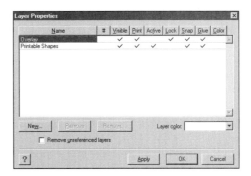

3.

Select the Visible property for the Overlay layer, and then click on OK on the Layer Properties dialog box to close it and view the drawing. The triangles and the title block disappear from the drawing, because they were on the deleted Nonprinting Shapes layer.

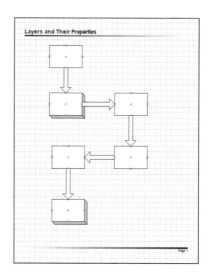

Part II

Projects

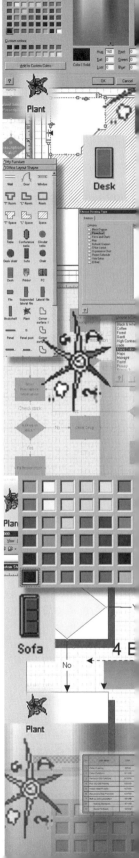

Chapter 10
Laying Out A Room

Project 1: Use one of Visio 2000's most valuable templates to specify a room

Project 2: Add furniture to your room

Project 3: Figure the cost of the furniture in your room

Planning Ahead

One of the most useful things you can do with Visio 2000 is to plan the furniture layout of a room. This is especially true if you are going to purchase new furniture; you need to calculate the cost and evaluate the number of pieces that will fit in the room. It can be an expensive mistake to purchase furniture, perhaps spend days assembling it, and then discover that you can't fit it all into the room. A few hours spent working with Visio 2000 can save you time, money, and headaches later.

Project 1: Specifying The Room Size

The first step in planning a furniture layout is to set up the dimensions of the room. This effort includes not only specifying the room's shape and size, but also adding important structural elements, such as doors, windows, and closets. After all, you'd look pretty silly placing a desk in front of the closet or cutting off all the light in the room by placing a big hutch in front of the window.

1.

To start working on the room design, you need to use the office layout feature; select File| New|Office Layout|Office Layout.

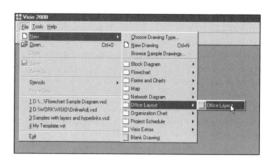

2.

This opens a new office layout template, complete with all the tools you need for laying out the room and adding furniture. Notice that the rulers (if you have them turned on) are calibrated in feet, and the scale is set to display a reasonably sized room.

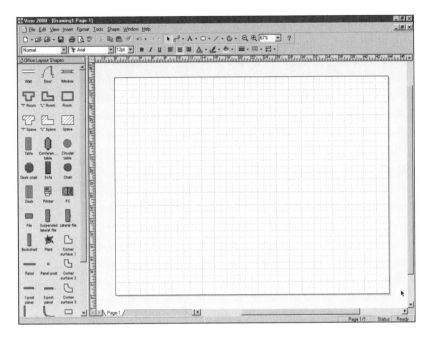

3.

Because the room you are laying out is not anywhere near this big, you are going to change the scale. Select File|Page Setup and click on the Drawing Scale tab. From the Pre-defined Scale drop-down menu, choose $^1/_2"$=1'0".

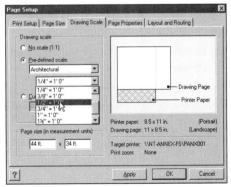

4.

Click on the Page Properties tab and enter "My Office" in the Name field.

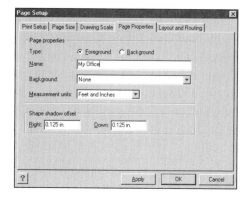

5.

Click on OK to close the Page Setup dialog box and view the new settings.

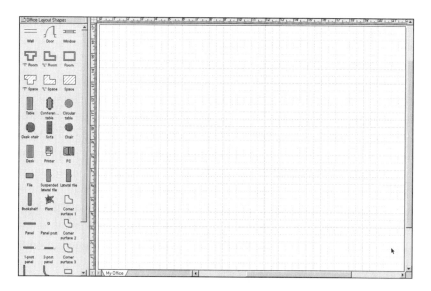

6.

Save your work at this point, and name the file "My Office Layout".

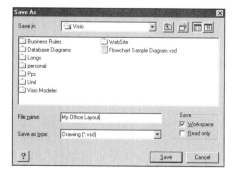

7.

Move the mouse pointer over the edge of the
vertical ruler, hold down the Ctrl key, and drag
the zero point of the horizontal ruler away
from the left edge of the paper.

Move the mouse pointer over the edge of the
horizontal ruler, hold down the Ctrl key, and
drag the zero point of the vertical ruler away
from the bottom edge of the paper.

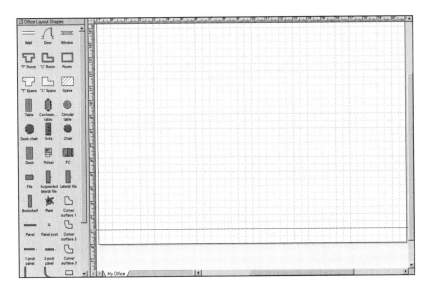

8.

Drag the rectangular room shape onto the diagram, positioning its lower-left corner at the
zero point of both rulers.

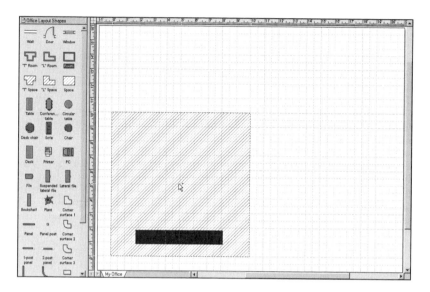

9.

Click and drag the upper, vertical, blue guide
to resize the vertical room dimension to 12'.

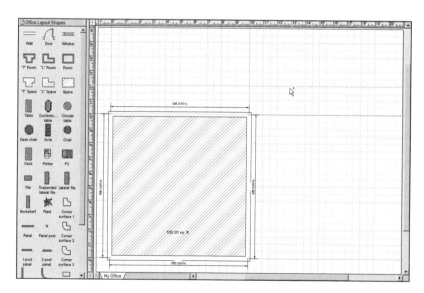

10.

This action moves the upper horizontal wall and redraws the dimensions for the vertical walls.

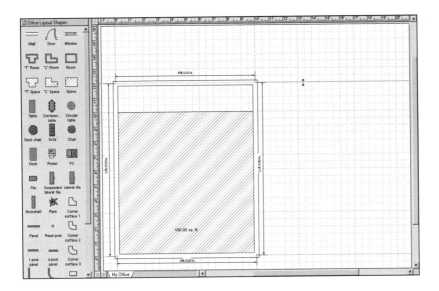

11.

Click and drag the right blue guide to resize the horizontal room dimension to 13'. This action moves the right vertical wall and redraws the dimensions for the horizontal walls.

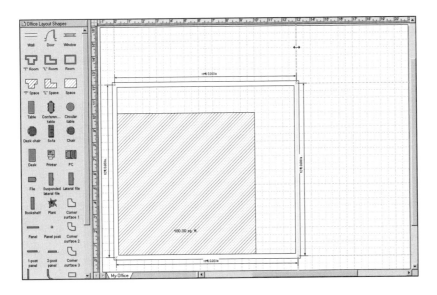

12.

Right-click on the hatched area that displays
the area of the room (in square feet), and
choose Auto Size from the shortcut menu. This
expands the area to fill the room.

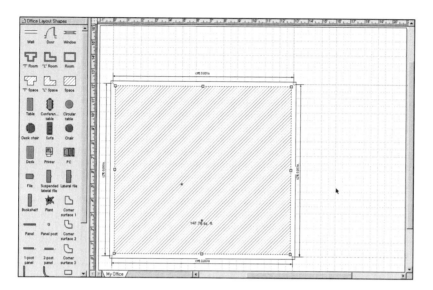

13.

Drag the door shape from the stencil until it is close to the bottom-right corner, making sure that the door itself overlaps the right wall.

When you release the mouse button, the door should "snap" into the corner.

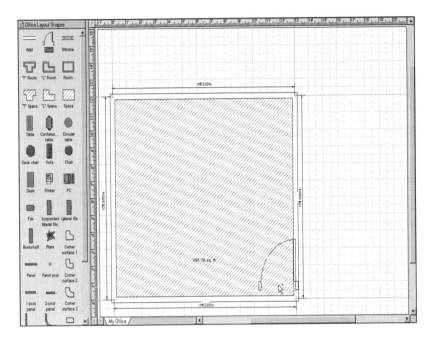

14.

Right-click on the door and choose Properties from the shortcut menu. Select a 36 in. Door Width from the drop-down menu in the Custom Properties dialog box.

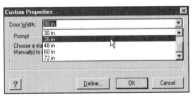

15.

Be sure the door object is still selected, and press
the left-arrow key five times to move the door
back inside the room (when you resized it, it
ended up inside a wall).

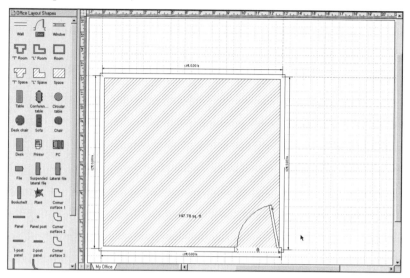

16.

Now you'll add some windows to allow light
into the office. The first window will be on the
left wall (12' vertical wall). Click and drag the
window shape from the stencil and position it
so it is overlapping the left wall.

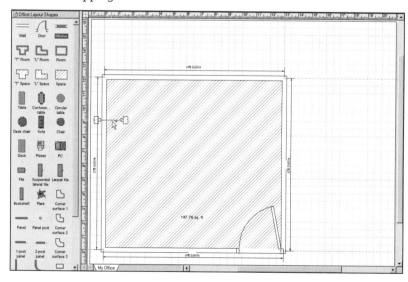

17.

The window automatically pivots to align with
the wall (neat, huh?). Click and drag the window until its center point is even with the 6' mark
on the vertical ruler. Notice the dotted line that
appears in the ruler as you drag the window.
This line helps you position the window correctly.

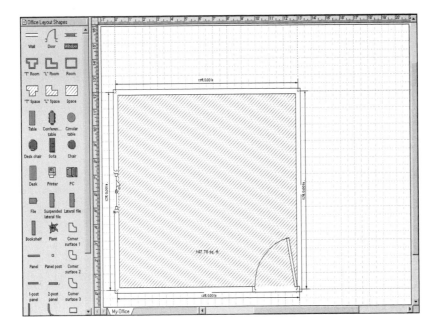

18.

Click on the small green rectangle at the lower
end of the window shape, and drag it until it
is even with the 3' mark on the vertical ruler.
Notice how the upper edge of the window also
moves, keeping the window centered.

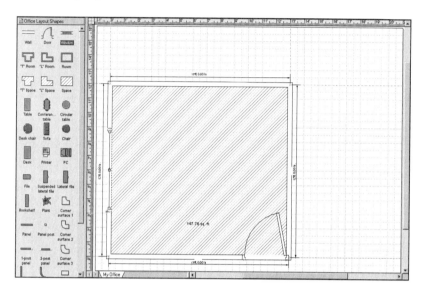

19.

Drag another window shape onto the upper
horizontal wall centered on the 6.5' mark on
the horizontal ruler.

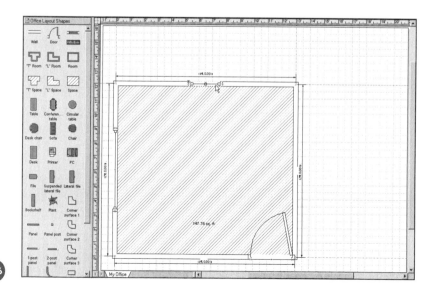

20.

Right-click on the window shape and choose Properties from the shortcut menu.

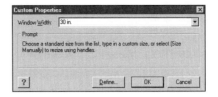

21.

Choose 72 in. from the Window Width drop-down menu to increase the size of the window. Then click on OK.

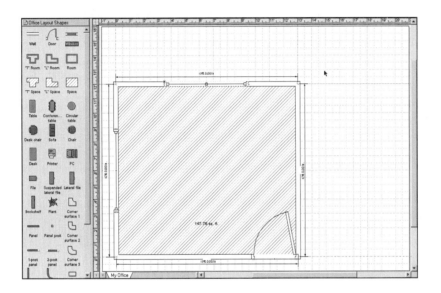

22.

Now you're going to add a closet. Because there is no closet shape in the template, you'll have to build one. Choose the Rectangle drawing tool from the toolbar, and drag a rectangle on the right vertical wall that extends from the 9' mark down to the 3' mark in the vertical ruler. Make sure the rectangle extends a little bit into the room.

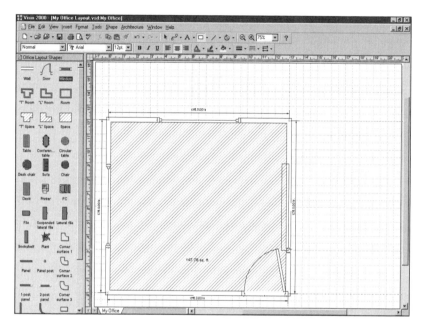

23.

Right-click on the "closet" rectangle and choose Format|Fill from the shortcut menu. Select a light blue fill color from the Color drop-down menu in the Fill section.

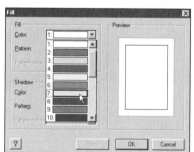

24.

Click on OK to apply the fill color.

Make sure the rectangle is still selected, then choose an 18 pt. font from the text toolbar.

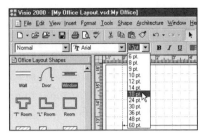

25.

Type the word "Closet" to label the shape. Click on the Bold button on the toolbar to make the text bold.

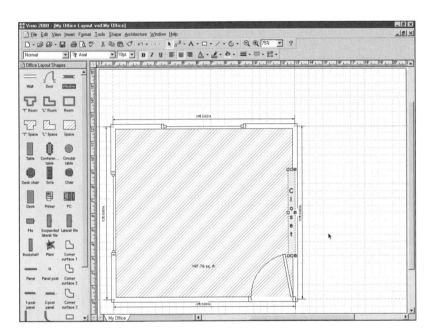

26.

It sure wouldn't do to place furniture in front of the light switch, so you'd better mark it. Drag the light switch symbol off the stencil and drop it on the wall by the door.

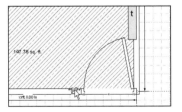

27.

Drag some electrical outlets onto the walls around the room as well, and place them according to the diagram. Because they are so small, use the sizing handles to increase their size and make them more visible.

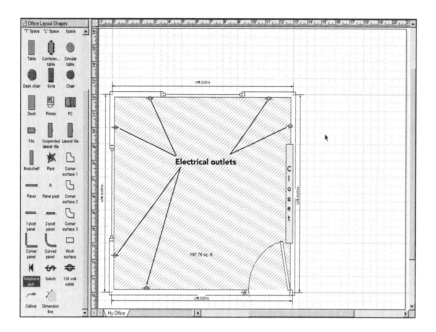

28.

Add a phone jack to the left vertical wall at the 9'6" mark. And that is our room!

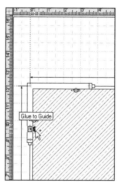

Project 2: Adding Furniture

Of course an empty room would be pretty difficult to work in, so let's add some furniture to the room. This layout might be just perfect for you, however, you might want to try various layouts before finding one you really like.

Adding A New Template

First, you need to add a new, empty stencil to this diagram. The reason for this: the furniture in the Office Layout Shapes stencil is not the right size. Each furniture vendor produces desks, laterals, bookshelves, and chairs in slightly different sizes. To modify the size, drag a shape (for example, a desk) from the Office Layout Shapes stencil onto the drawing, size it to match the piece supplied by the vendor of your choice, and then drag that custom piece onto your new stencil, adding it to the stencil. That way, the next time you need a desk, you'll have one all sized and ready to go.

1.

To create a new stencil, select File|Stencils|New Stencil. This adds a blank stencil to your template.

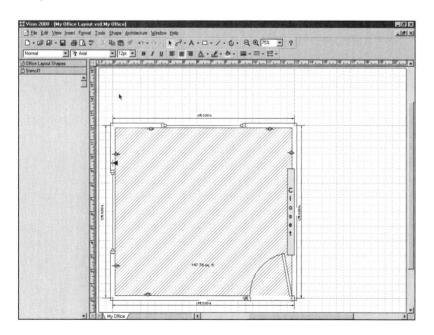

2.

Click in the upper-left corner of the new stencil, and choose Properties from the menu. This opens the stencil's Properties dialog box. Type "My Furniture" into the Title field.

3.

The disk icon in the upper-right corner of the stencil title bar indicates that a change has been made to the stencil that needs to be saved. Click on the disk icon.

4.

Enter the name "My Furniture" for the File
Name in the Save As dialog box, and click on
Save. Then click on the title bar of the Office
Layout Shapes stencil to make the stencil vis-
ible—you are now ready to start adding your
furniture.

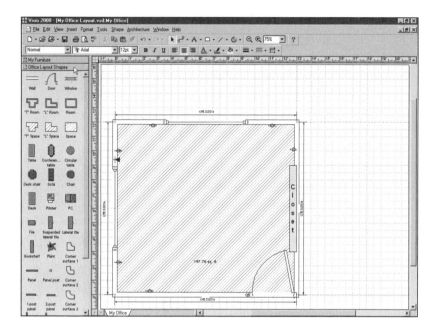

Positioning The Furniture

The first piece of furniture you are going to add is a desk. You'll have to adjust the size to match the furniture you're interested in buying.

1.

Drag the Desk shape onto the drawing, but put it outside the room.

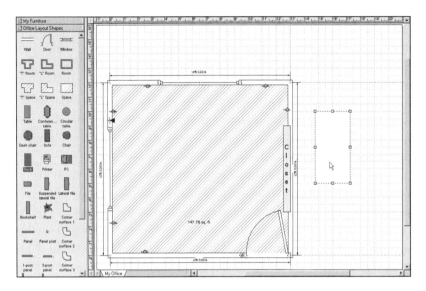

2.

Right-click on the desk shape and choose View|Size & Position from the shortcut menu. In the Size & Position window, enter the height as 26.75 in. and the width as 59.5 in. This corresponds to the dimensions of the nominal 60" desk.

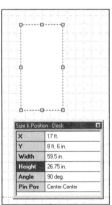

Size & Position - Desk	
X	17 ft.
Y	8 ft. 6 in.
Width	59.5 in.
Height	26.75 in.
Angle	90 deg.
Pin Pos	Center-Center

3.

If the "My Furniture" stencil is not editable, click on the title bar of the My Furniture stencil, and choose Edit from the menu (click on the icon in the upper-left corner to display the menu). Hold down the Ctrl key and drag the new desk onto the stencil. This adds the desk to the stencil *without* deleting it from the drawing.

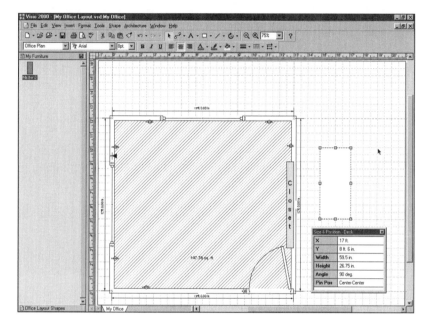

4.

Right-click on the new stencil shape, and choose Master Properties from the shortcut menu. Enter the new name "60 inch Desk".

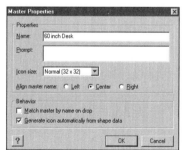

5.

Return to the desk shape, and adjust the width to 47.5 in. to create a 48 inch desk.

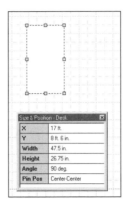

6.

Hold down the Ctrl key and drag the new desk onto the Stencil. Right-click on the new stencil shape, and choose Master Properties from the shortcut menu. Enter the new name "48 inch Desk".

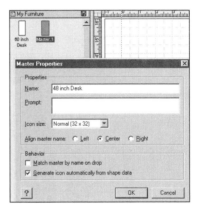

7.

Follow the previous steps to create a 36 inch desk with a width of 35.5 inches. Then delete the desk shape from the drawing.

You have one more shape to build—the corner surface. Click on the title bar of the Office Layout Shapes stencil and drag the Corner Surface 1 shape from the stencil onto the drawing, once again placing it outside the room area. The Size & Position window should still be visible and will now show the dimensions of the Corner Surface.

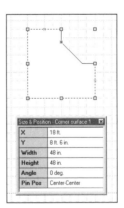

8.

Adjust both the width and height to 47.25 in.

Next, you need to adjust the dimension where the corner surface joins the desk because this dimension should match the width of the desk. Switch to the My Furniture stencil, drag the 36 inch desk onto the work area, and align it with the corner surface.

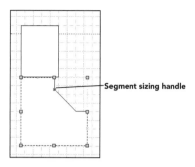

Segment sizing handle

9.

Grab the segment sizing handle and drag it to match the corner surface edge dimension of the desk width.

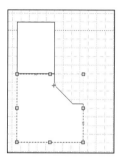

10.

Drag the corner surface onto the My Furniture stencil, and adjust the name to read "Corner Desk". Delete any extraneous shapes (such as the 36 inch desk) remaining on the drawing.

11.

Drag and drop the corner desk shape near the lower-left corner of the office.

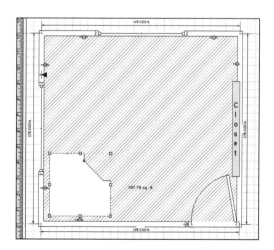

12.

Click on one of the electrical outlets in that corner, then Shift-click on the other one to select them both. Choose Shape|Bring to Front to ensure they will be visible when you move the corner desk all the way into the corner. Then drag the corner desk flush with the walls in the corner of the room.

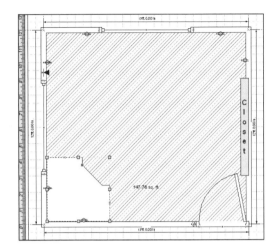

13.

Drag another corner desk from the stencil and place it near the upper-left corner of the room. Right-click on the shape, and choose Shape|Rotate Right.

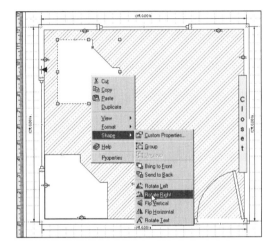

14.

This aligns the shape with the corner of the room.

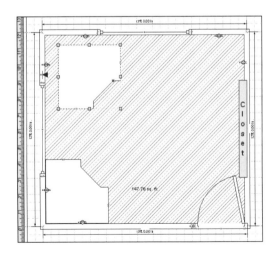

15.

Click on the two electrical outlets and the phone jack in the upper-left corner, and choose Shape|Bring To Front. Then, maneuver the corner desk into the upper-left corner.

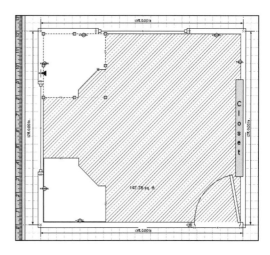

16.

Drag a 36 inch desk onto the screen and align it with the corner desk located in the upper-left corner of the room.

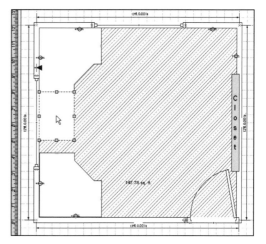

17.

Drag a 60 inch desk onto the drawing area. Right-click on the desk, and choose Shape|Rotate Right from the shortcut menu.

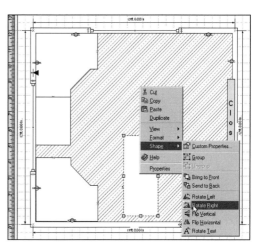

18.

Maneuver the desk against the lower wall, and align it with the corner desk.

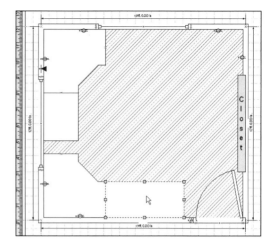

19.

Hold down the Ctrl key, click on the 60 inch desk, and drag a copy of it to the upper wall (under the window). Align it with the corner desk in the upper-left corner.

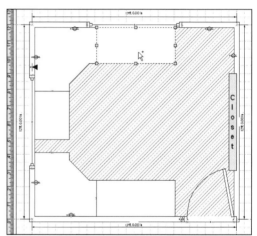

20.

Switch to the Office Furniture Shapes and drag two desk chairs onto the drawing—one at each corner desk.

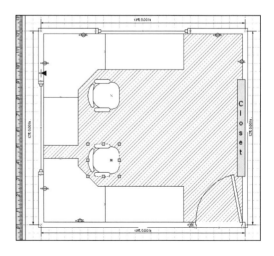

21.

Click on the rotation handle of the lower chair and drag it around to face the corner desk. Repeat this action with the other chair.

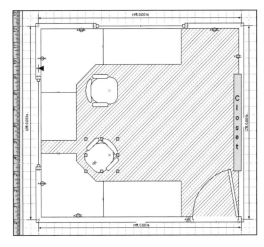

22.

Drag a File shape from the Office Layout Shapes stencil into the upper-right corner. Rotate the file (Shape|Rotate Right from the shortcut menu), and align it with the end of the desk. There is your office layout.

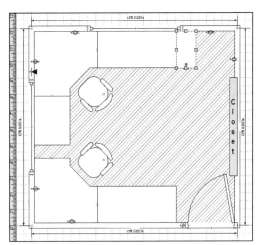

Project 3: Figuring The Cost

Now that you've got a furniture layout, you need to figure out what it is going to cost to equip your office. This section adds a Cost property to each shape and then calculates the total cost of the furniture.

Adding A New Property

Follow these steps to add a Cost property to each shape.

1.

Right-click on the File shape and choose Properties from the shortcut menu.

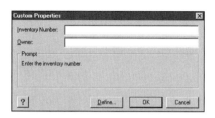

2.

Click on the Define button to bring up the Define Custom Properties dialog box, then click on New. Enter the name of the new property as "Cost".

3.

Choose Number from the Type drop-down menu and a format of Floating Pt (2.75).

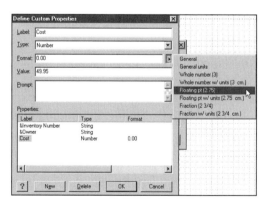

4.

Click on OK to add the new property to the Custom Properties dialog box for the File shape.

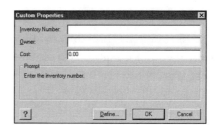

Enter the value 49.95 for the cost of the file, then click on OK. Repeat this task with each of the other shapes on the page, using the following costs:

- *60 inch desk (both of them)*—319.95 each

- *36 inch desk*—219.95

- *Corner desk (both of them)*—349.95 each

- *Desk chairs (both of them)*—179.95 each

Running A Property Report

Follow these steps to run a property report and calculate the cost of your furniture.

1.

Select Tools|Property Report. Click on the Next button in the Property Reporting Wizard to move to the next panel. Choose the Shapes You Select Yourself radio button so you can include just the shapes that have a Cost property.

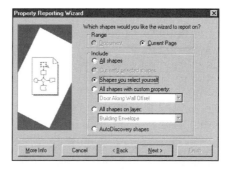

2.

Click on the Next button. This panel enables you to name the layer on which to place the selected shapes. Enter "Cost Report Shapes" for the layer name.

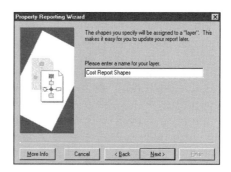

3.

Click on the Next button. This panel enables you to choose the shapes you want to include on the report. If necessary, move the panel out of the way, click on the first shape, and Shift-click on the other shapes to add them to the collection.

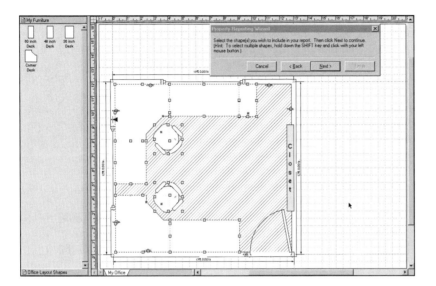

4.

Click on the Next button. Choose Cost from the Properties list and click on the right-arrow button to move the Cost property into the Include list.

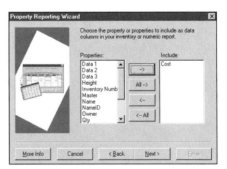

5.

Click on the Next button. Because the type of report you want is a Total report (the default), you don't have to change anything in this wizard panel.

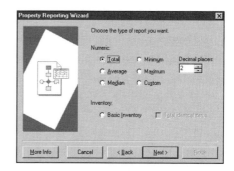

6.

Click on the Next button. This panel displays a list of all the shapes, their individual costs, and the total cost of the items.

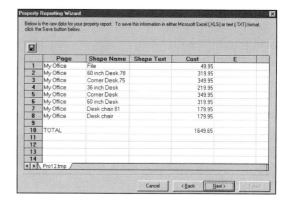

	Page	Shape Name	Shape Text	Cost	E
1	My Office	File		49.95	
2	My Office	60 inch Desk.78		319.95	
3	My Office	Corner Desk.75		349.95	
4	My Office	36 inch Desk		219.95	
5	My Office	Corner Desk		349.95	
6	My Office	60 inch Desk		319.95	
7	My Office	Desk chair.81		179.95	
8	My Office	Desk chair		179.95	
9					
10	TOTAL			1649.65	
11					
12					
13					
14					

7.

Click on the Next button. In this panel, adjust the label text to read "Furniture Cost".

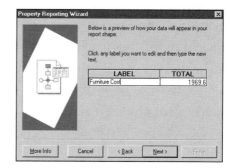

LABEL	TOTAL
Furniture Cost	1969.6

8.

Click on the Next button. This panel enables you to enter the title that will appear in the embedded report object in your diagram, as well as select which drawing page it will appear on. Enter "Total Cost Report" for the title.

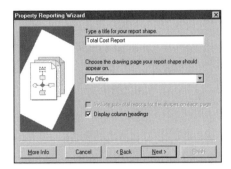

9.

Click on the Next button. Select the items you want included in your report object. Select the Visio Filename checkbox and the Purpose Of Report checkbox. Enter "Calculate Total Furniture Cost" as the purpose.

10.

Click on OK. Then click on the Finish button to place the cost report object in the drawing.

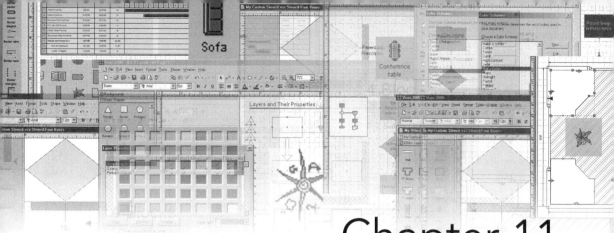

Chapter 11
Building An
Organization Chart

Project 1: Create a file that contains organization information

Project 2: Tell the Organization Chart Wizard how to build your organization chart

Project 3: Modify the organization chart

Company Structure

Most organizations that consist of more than a few people have an organization chart that shows the structure of the company. While it is certainly possible to build an organization chart using Visio 2000 (a template is included for just that purpose), it is usually more efficient to maintain organization information in a file. It is easier to update a file, especially since you don't have to worry about laying out the chart on a piece of paper or learning a new tool (even an easy tool like Visio 2000). Now you have the best of both worlds—the ability to maintain your organization information in a file and create a Visio organization chart automatically from the contents of that file. This chapter shows you how to build a Microsoft Excel file and use it to create an organization chart.

Project 1: Building The File

Although the Visio 2000 Organization Chart Wizard can build an organization chart from a variety of file types, the easiest way to maintain and use a file is to create a spreadsheet. With the proper column identifications (detailed in this section), creating an organization chart from a spreadsheet is very straightforward.

This chapter assumes you use Microsoft Excel as your spreadsheet application. If you don't, you can usually use another spreadsheet program and save the file as a Microsoft Excel file.

1.

To create the file, open a new, blank spreadsheet.

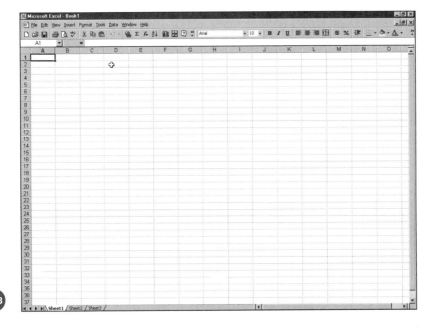

2.

Enter the column headings in the first row of the spreadsheet: "Name", "Position", "Reports_To", "Department", and "Telephone".

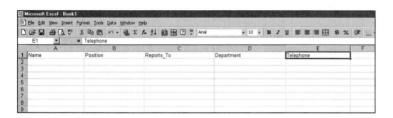

3.

Select all the cells in the first row that contain entries, and choose Format Cells from the shortcut menu. Select the Alignment tab, and choose Center from the Horizontal drop-down menu.

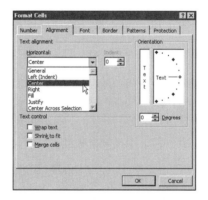

4.

Choose the Border tab in the Format Cells dialog box, and click on both the Outline button and the Inside button.

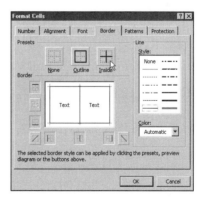

5.

You can also add a background color to the header cells from the Patterns tab. Your spreadsheet should now look like the graphic shown here.

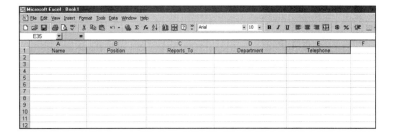

6.

Add some sample data to your spreadsheet, or fill it out with your own organization's information. Then, save your file as "Org Chart Wizard Example.xls".

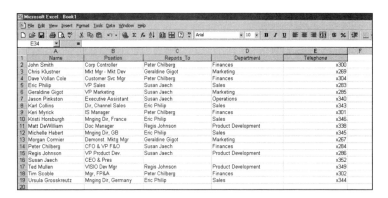

Project 2: Using The Organization Chart Wizard

Once you have defined your data file, you can use the Visio 2000 Organization Chart Wizard to build an organization chart from that data. Thereafter, you can update the chart from the file whenever you need to. This section discusses using the Organization Chart Wizard.

1.

To start the Organization Chart Wizard, select File|New|Organization Chart, and choose Organization Chart Wizard.

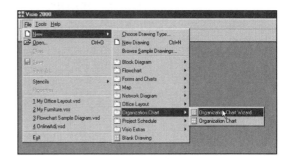

2.

The first panel of the Organization Chart Wizard opens. Be sure to select the radio button labeled Information That's Already Stored In A File Or Database.

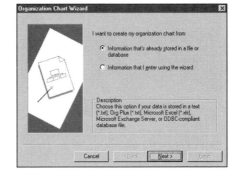

3.

Click on the Next button. In this panel, select the radio button labeled A Text, Org Plus (*.txt), Or Microsoft Excel File.

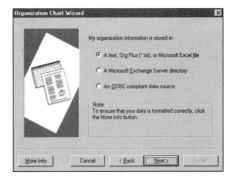

4.

Click on the Next button. In this panel, choose the Excel file that contains the organization data. Click on the Browse button if you need to select the file from the standard open file dialog box.

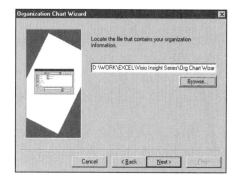

5.

Click on the Next button. In this panel, choose the spreadsheet column that corresponds to the person's name (Name) and to whom they report (Reports_To) from the drop-down menus. Notice that Visio 2000 automatically selects the correct spreadsheet columns based on the column headings in row one of the spreadsheet. Visio is able to do this because of the way you named the columns.

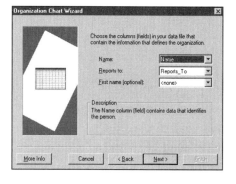

6.

Click on the Next button. In this panel, use the drop-down menus to choose the fields to display on the First Line and Second Line of each box in the organization chart.

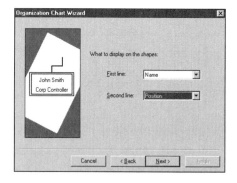

7.

Click on the Next button. In this panel, choose the information you want added to the organization chart shapes as custom properties. In this example, just choose Department and Telephone, then click on the Add button. Name and Position are already displayed, and the Reports_To relationship will be shown by the structure of the diagram.

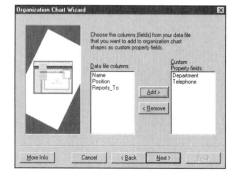

8.

Click on the Next button. In this panel, let the wizard decide how to break your organization across multiple pages by selecting the second radio button.

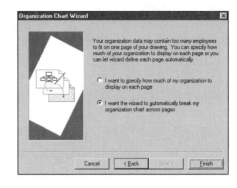

9.

Click on the Finish button. Visio 2000 lays out the organization chart for you.

All entries in the Reports_To field must refer to a valid entry in a Name field of another record, or an error will result. The Names are case-sensitive, so be careful when entering them.

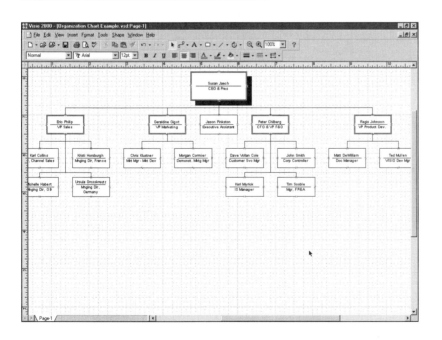

Project 3: Modifying The Chart

Visio 2000 does a pretty good job of laying out an organization chart, but you may wish to customize the results yourself. Visio provides plenty of tools for changing an organization chart. This section demonstrates some of those tools.

1.

To improve the layout of the organization chart on the page, you'll use the Organization Chart toolbar.

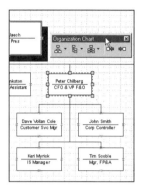

2.

Click on the box for Peter Chilberg. Choose the drop-down menu on the Organization Chart toolbar that controls stacked shapes.

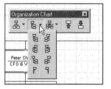

3.

Choose the third button down on the left side of the menu, and click on it. This stacks the subordinates of Peter Chilborg in an efficient pattern.

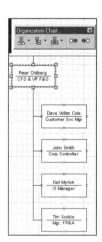

4.

Select Eric Philips, and right-click on the shape to display the shortcut menu.

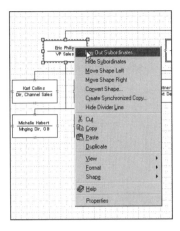

5.

Choose Lay Out Subordinates from the short-cut menu.

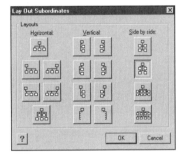

6.

Choose the top-left button in the Vertical section. This stacks the subordinates of Eric Philips in a slightly different pattern from the one used earlier.

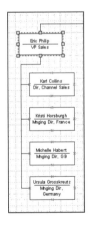

7.

Next, you're going to add subordinates to Matt DeWilliam. To do so, you need to convert him to a manager (actually, you don't *have* to, but it is better to do so). Right-click on Matt DeWilliam and choose Convert Shape from the shortcut menu.

8.

Choose the Manager shape and click on OK.

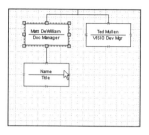

Be sure that Matt DeWilliam is still selected, and choose the Connector tool from the toolbar. Then click on the Position shape in the stencil, and drag it onto the page below Matt DeWilliam.

9.

Repeat this action to give Matt two subordinates. Fill in their names and titles: "Joe Smith", "Assistant Doc Manager", and "Jeremy Sampson", "Assistant Doc Manager".

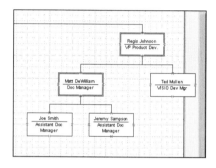

10.

Notice how this action pushed poor Ted Mullen clear off the page! To fix this, click on Matt DeWilliam, and choose the stacked shape button on the Organization Chart toolbar. Choose the bottom-left shape.

11.

The shapes are now rearranged so everything fits on the page once again.

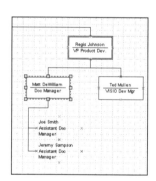

Chapter 12
Building A Timeline

Project 1: Learn to use Visio's special facilities to build a timeline for a construction job

Project 2: Customize and print your timeline

Beyond Drawing

Visio isn't just for drawing pictures! In this chapter, you're going to create a project-planning timeline to remodel the office you designed for your furniture layout in Chapter 10.

Project 1: Building A Gantt Chart

A Gantt chart is a special type of timeline. The shapes in a Gantt chart have their own behavior. You can connect tasks so that one task does not start until another finishes and add milestones. You can also adjust the start date, end date, and duration of a task; Visio will adjust the dependent tasks to compensate.

1.

To start the process of building a Gantt chart, select File|New|Project Schedule|Gantt Chart.

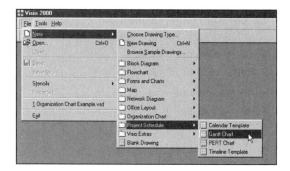

2.

This opens the Gantt Chart Options dialog box.

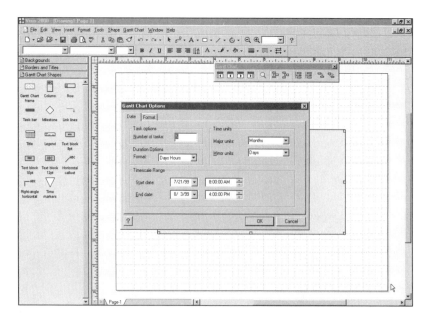

3.

Enter "8" into the Number Of Tasks field. Set the start date by clicking on the drop arrow adjacent to the Start date field.

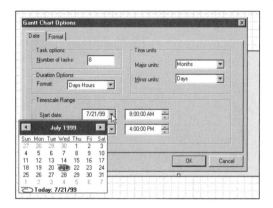

4.

Click on the right arrow at the top of the calendar to advance to September, and choose September 6 as the start date for the project.

Then, choose the end date as 10/31/99.

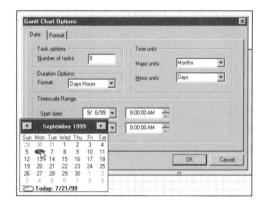

5.

Switch to the Format tab of the Gantt Chart Options dialog box.

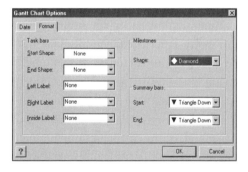

6.

Choose Resource Name from the Right Label drop-down menu. The assigned resource will appear alongside the task bar in the final chart.

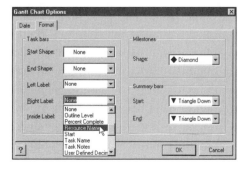

7.

Click on OK to create the template for the Gantt chart.

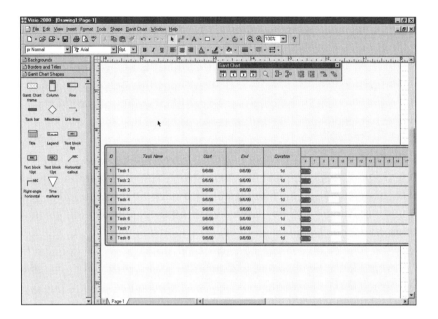

8.

At this point, you'll need to adjust the working options. Right-click on the frame around the outside of the Gantt chart and choose Configure Working Time from the shortcut menu.

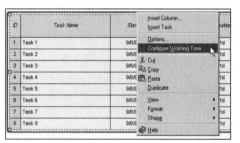

9.

This displays the Configure Working Time dialog box.

Because the work crew will also be working on Saturdays, select the Saturday checkbox. Otherwise, any task that you draw that starts or ends on a Saturday will automatically be advanced to the next working day (as it will be with Sundays as well). Click on OK to close the dialog box.

10.

You also need to add some additional columns to track work progress. Right-click on the Gantt chart frame again and choose Insert Column from the shortcut menu. This opens the Insert Column dialog box.

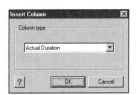

11.

Choose Actual Start from the Column Type drop-down menu and click on OK. Repeat this action to add an Actual End column as well. These columns are added to the right of the Gantt chart.

If you'd rather have the new columns added to the left of the Gantt chart, click on each column and drag it from the right end to the left end. As long as you drop the column somewhere inside the Gantt chart, the column will be inserted into the chart. You can rearrange the columns using this same method.

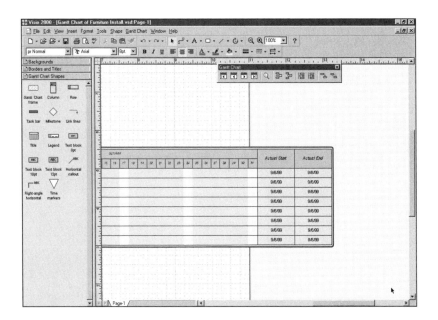

12.

To start specifying the tasks, click on the Task 1 box in the Task Name column. Enter the name of the task as "Order Flooring".

ID	Task Name	Start	End	Duration										
					6	7	8	9	10	11	12	13	14	15
1	Order Flooring	9/6/99	9/6/99	1d										
2	Task 2	9/6/99	9/6/99	1d										
3	Task 3	9/6/99	9/6/99	1d										
4	Task 4	9/6/99	9/6/99	1d										
5	Task 5	9/6/99	9/6/99	1d										
6	Task 6	9/6/99	9/6/99	1d										
7	Task 7	9/6/99	9/6/99	1d										
8	Task 8	9/6/99	9/6/99	1d										

13.

Double-click on the End column and enter 9/20/99 as the end date for the task. Notice how Visio 2000 automatically extends the task bar to 9/20/99 and calculates the Duration.

ID	Task Name	Start	End	Duration	Sep '99
1	Order Flooring	9/6/99	9/20/99	13d	
2	Task 2	9/6/99	9/6/99	1d	
3	Task 3	9/6/99	9/6/99	1d	
4	Task 4	9/6/99	9/6/99	1d	
5	Task 5	9/6/99	9/6/99	1d	
6	Task 6	9/6/99	9/6/99	1d	
7	Task 7	9/6/99	9/6/99	1d	
8	Task 8	9/6/99	9/6/99	1d	

14.

Right-click on the task line and choose Shape|Custom Properties from the shortcut menu. This displays the Custom Properties dialog box.

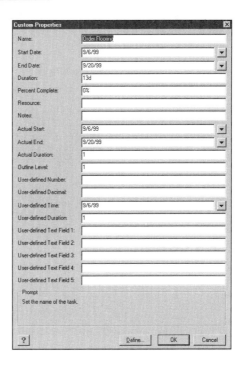

15.

Enter "Bobo Flooring" into the Resource field, and click on OK. This places the resource name to the right of the task bar because you specified earlier that the right label for the task bar should show the resource name.

ID	Task Name	Start	End	Duration	Sep '99
1	Order Flooring	9/6/99	9/20/99	13d	Bobo Flooring
2	Task 2	9/6/99	9/6/99	1d	
3	Task 3	9/6/99	9/6/99	1d	
4	Task 4	9/6/99	9/6/99	1d	
5	Task 5	9/6/99	9/6/99	1d	
6	Task 6	9/6/99	9/6/99	1d	
7	Task 7	9/6/99	9/6/99	1d	
8	Task 8	9/6/99	9/6/99	1d	

16.

Specify the Task 2 name as "Order Furniture". Set a Start date of 9/10/99. Then, click on the task bar, grab the sizing handle on the right, and drag it to 9/20/99.

Task Name	Start	End	Duration
r Flooring	9/6/99	9/20/99	13d
r Furniture	9/10/99	9/10/99	1d
3	9/6/99	9/6/99	1d
4	9/6/99	9/6/99	1d
5	9/6/99	9/6/99	1d
6	9/6/99	9/6/99	1d
7	9/6/99	9/6/99	1d
8	9/6/99	9/6/99	1d

17.

Notice how Visio 2000 recalculates both the End date and the Duration to match the length of the task bar.

Task Name	Start	End	Duration
r Flooring	9/6/99	9/20/99	13d
r Furniture	9/10/99	9/20/99	9d
3	9/6/99	9/6/99	1d
4	9/6/99	9/6/99	1d
5	9/6/99	9/6/99	1d
6	9/6/99	9/6/99	1d
7	9/6/99	9/6/99	1d
8	9/6/99	9/6/99	1d

18.

Set the Resource field (Custom Properties dialog box) to be "Online Furniture".

Specify Task 3 as "Remove Old Furniture". Click on the task bar, and drag it until the right end is even with 9/20/99. Notice how the Start date and End date are adjusted automatically to match the new location of the task bar.

k Name	Start	End	Duration	
	9/6/99	9/20/99	13d	Bobo Flooring
	9/10/99	9/20/99	9d	Online Furniture
ture	9/20/99	9/20/99	1d	
	9/6/99	9/6/99	1d	
	9/6/99	9/6/99	1d	
	9/6/99	9/6/99	1d	
	9/6/99	9/6/99	1d	
	9/6/99	9/6/99	1d	

19.

Set the Resource field to be "Joe's Furniture Movers".

Specify Task 4 as "Pull Up Old Flooring". Because you can't pull up the old flooring until you remove the furniture (which was Task 3), you need to establish a link between these two tasks. To do so, click on the Remove Old Furniture task bar, then hold down the Shift key and click on the Pull Up Old Flooring task bar.

Task Name	Start	End	Duration	Sep1 ###
Order Flooring	9/6/99	9/20/99	13d	Bobo Flooring
Order Furniture	9/10/99	9/20/99	9d	Online Furniture
Remove Old Furniture	9/20/99	9/20/99	1d	Joe's Furniture Movers
Pull Up Old Flooring	9/6/99	9/6/99	1d	
Task 5	9/6/99	9/6/99	1d	
Task 6	9/6/99	9/6/99	1d	
Task 7	9/6/99	9/6/99	1d	
Task 8	9/6/99	9/6/99	1d	

20.

Choose the Link Tasks button from the Gantt Chart toolbar.

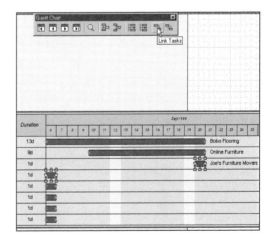

21.

The two tasks are now linked: The second task will start automatically after the first task is complete.

Task Name	Start	End	Duration	Sep1 ###
Order Flooring	9/6/99	9/20/99	13d	Bobo Flooring
Order Furniture	9/10/99	9/20/00	9d	Online Furniture
Remove Old Furniture	9/20/99	9/20/99	1d	Joe's Furniture Movers
Pull Up Old Flooring	9/21/99	9/21/99	1d	
Task 5	9/6/99	9/6/99	1d	
Task 6	9/6/99	9/6/99	1d	
Task 7	9/6/99	9/6/99	1d	
Task 8	9/6/99	9/6/99	1d	

22.

Change the duration of the task Remove Old Furniture to two days (enter "2d" into the Duration column). Notice how the task bar gets longer and how the Pull Up Old Flooring task is automatically delayed.

Task Name	Start	End	Duration	Sept 999
Order Flooring	9/6/99	9/20/99	13d	Bobo Flooring
Order Furniture	9/10/99	9/20/99	9d	Online Furniture
Remove Old Furniture	9/20/99	9/21/99	2d	Joe's Furniture Mo
Pull Up Old Flooring	9/22/99	9/22/99	1d	
Task 5	9/6/99	9/6/99	1d	
Task 6	9/6/99	9/6/99	1d	
Task 7	9/6/99	9/6/99	1d	
Task 8	9/6/99	9/6/99	1d	

23.

Set the Resource field to be "Bobo Flooring".

Specify Task 5 as "Install New Flooring", and change the duration to four days (boy, these guys are *slow*). Link the previous task (Pull Up Old Flooring) to this one. The elapsed time for the task is actually five days, because one of the days is a Sunday (a nonworking day, identified by the yellow bar).

Task Name	Start	End	Duration	Sept 999
rg	9/6/99	9/20/99	13d	Bobo Flooring
ure	9/10/99	9/20/99	9d	Online Furniture
Furniture	9/20/99	9/21/99	2d	Joe's Furniture Movers
looring	9/22/99	9/22/99	1d	Bobo Flooring
Flooring	9/23/99	9/27/99	4d	
	9/6/99	9/6/99	1d	
	9/6/99	9/6/99	1d	
	9/6/99	9/6/99	1d	

24.

Set the Resource field to be "Bobo Flooring".

Specify Task 6 as "Assemble New Furniture", change the duration to three days, and set the Resource field to be "Bobo Flooring". Link the previous task (Install New Flooring) to this task.

Start	End	Duration	
9/6/99	9/20/99	13d	Bobo Flooring
9/10/99	9/20/99	9d	Online Furniture
9/20/99	9/21/99	2d	Joe's Furniture Movers
9/22/99	9/22/99	1d	Bobo Flooring
9/23/99	9/27/99	4d	Bobo Flooring
9/27/99	9/29/99	3d	Bobo Flooring
9/6/99	9/6/99	1d	
9/6/99	9/6/99	1d	

25.

It doesn't look like you're going to need Task 7, so right-click on the ID for Task 7, and choose Delete Task from the shortcut menu.

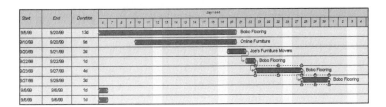

26.

Specify Task 8 as "Set up new computer", and change the duration to two days. Then, link this task to the previous one (Assemble New Furniture). Set the Resource field to be "Owner".

Start	End	Duration	
9/6/99	9/20/99	13d	Bobo Flooring
9/10/99	9/20/99	9d	Online Furniture
9/20/99	9/21/99	2d	Joe's Furniture Movers
9/22/99	9/22/99	1d	Bobo Flooring
9/23/99	9/27/99	4d	Bobo Flooring
9/27/99	9/29/99	3d	Bobo Flooring
10/1/99	10/2/99	2d	Owner

27.

Choose Gantt Chart|Options to display the Gantt Chart Options dialog box, and change the End date to 10/08/99.

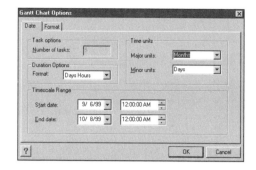

28.

Now you're going to try to estimate the last task (Set up new computer) by breaking it into two subtasks: Setting Up Hardware and Installing Software. To do so, right-click on the ID column for the last task (Set up new computer) and choose Insert Task from the shortcut menu.

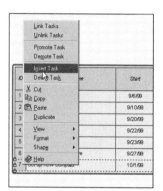

29.

Repeat this action to add another new, blank task.

ID	Task Name	Start	End	Duration
1	Order Flooring	9/6/99	9/20/99	13d
2	Order Furniture	9/10/99	9/20/99	9d
3	Remove Old Furniture	9/20/99	9/21/99	2d
4	Pull Up Old Flooring	9/22/99	9/22/99	1d
5	Install New Flooring	9/23/99	9/27/99	4d
6	Assemble New Furniture	9/27/99	9/29/99	3d
7				
8				
9	Set up new computer	10/1/99	10/2/99	2d

30.

Click in the ID column of the first blank task, and drag it below the Set up new computer task.

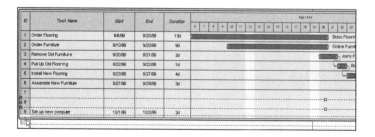

31.

Repeat this maneuver by dragging the other blank task below the Set up new computer task.

ID	Task Name	Start	End	Duration	Sep 1999
1	Order Flooring	9/6/99	9/20/99	13d	Bobo F
2	Order Furniture	9/10/99	9/20/99	9d	Online
3	Remove Old Furniture	9/20/99	9/21/99	2d	Jo
4	Pull Up Old Flooring	9/22/99	9/22/99	1d	
5	Install New Flooring	9/23/99	9/27/99	4d	
6	Assemble New Furniture	9/27/99	9/29/99	3d	
7	Set up new computer	10/1/99	10/2/99	2d	
8					
9					

32.

Click in the first blank task and label the task "Set Up Hardware". Set the duration to 12h (12 hours). Visio 2000 automatically converts the time to days and hours, the default option for displaying time.

ID	Task Name	Start	End	Duration	
1	Order Flooring	9/6/99	9/20/99	13d	
2	Order Furniture	9/10/99	9/20/99	9d	
3	Remove Old Furniture	9/20/99	9/21/99	2d	
4	Pull Up Old Flooring	9/22/99	9/22/99	1d	
5	Install New Flooring	9/23/99	9/27/99	4d	
6	Assemble New Furniture	9/27/99	9/29/99	3d	
7	Set up new computer	10/1/99	10/2/99	2d	
8	Set Up Hardware	9/6/99	9/7/99	1d 4h	
9					

To change the time display format, right-click on the frame around the outside of the Gantt chart, and choose Gantt Chart Options from the shortcut menu. The resulting dialog box enables you to specify how Visio displays time.

33.

Click in the next blank task and label it "Install Software". Set the duration to 16h for this task.

ID	Task Name	Start	End	Duration	
1	Order Flooring	9/6/99	9/20/99	13d	
2	Order Furniture	9/10/99	9/20/99	9d	
3	Remove Old Furniture	9/20/99	9/21/99	2d	
4	Pull Up Old Flooring	9/22/99	9/22/99	1d	
5	Install New Flooring	9/23/99	9/27/99	4d	
6	Assemble New Furniture	9/27/99	9/29/99	3d	
7	Set up new computer	10/1/99	10/2/99	2d	
8	Set Up Hardware	9/6/99	9/7/99	1d 4h	
9	Install Software	9/6/99	9/7/99	2d	

34.

Link the two tasks: Set Up Hardware is the first task, followed by Install Software.

ID	Task Name	Start	End	Duration	
1	Order Flooring	9/6/99	9/20/99	13d	
2	Order Furniture	9/10/99	9/20/99	9d	
3	Remove Old Furniture	9/20/99	9/21/99	2d	
4	Pull Up Old Flooring	9/22/99	9/22/99	1d	
5	Install New Flooring	9/23/99	9/27/99	4d	
6	Assemble New Furniture	9/27/99	9/29/99	3d	
7	Set up new computer	10/1/99	10/2/99	2d	
8	Set Up Hardware	9/6/99	9/7/99	1d 4h	
9	Install Software	9/7/99	9/8/99	2d	

35.

With these two tasks still selected, choose Gantt Chart|Demote Task from the menu. The two tasks become components of the task above them, which happens to be the Set up new computer task. Visio adjusts the duration of the overall task (which is still called Set up new computer) to match the durations of the subtasks. It also adjusts the subtasks to start at the beginning of the overall task.

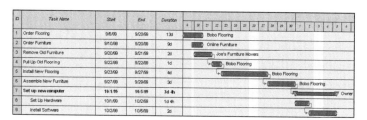

ID	Task Name	Start	End	Duration																	
1	Order Flooring	9/6/99	9/20/99	13d		Bobo Flooring															
2	Order Furniture	9/10/99	9/20/99	9d		Online Furniture															
3	Remove Old Furniture	9/20/99	9/21/99	2d		Joe's Furniture Movers															
4	Pull Up Old Flooring	9/22/99	9/22/99	1d		Bobo Flooring															
5	Install New Flooring	9/23/99	9/27/99	4d		Bobo Flooring															
6	Assemble New Furniture	9/27/99	9/29/99	3d		Bobo Flooring															
7	Set up new computer	10/1/99	10/5/99	3d 4h		Owner															
8	Set Up Hardware	10/1/99	10/2/99	1d 4h																	
9	Install Software	10/2/99	10/5/99	2d																	

Project 2: Printing And Customizing The Chart

The timeline you built in the previous project is quite large: It won't fit on a standard piece of paper without shrinking it to a size you can hardly read. In this section, you will adjust the timeline to fit on a larger piece of paper and add some adornments to give it a more professional look.

1.

Select File|Page Setup to display the Page Setup dialog box. Notice that the printer paper does not line up with the landscape orientation of the Visio drawing.

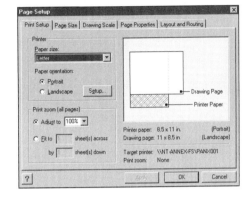

2.

To fix this problem, select the Landscape radio button in the Printer section of the dialog box.

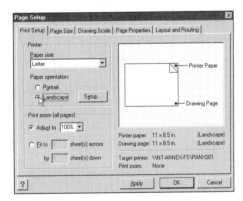

3.

Switch to the Page Size tab and click on the second drop-down menu under the Pre-Defined Size radio button to display the page sizes.

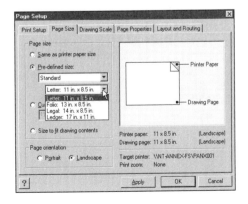

4.

Choose 14 in. x 8.5 in. (legal) as the page size, then click on OK. Shrink the diagram to 50% to view the overall relationship between the timeline and the page.

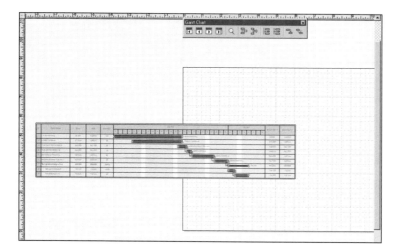

5.

Drag the timeline onto the paper and center it on the page. You may need to resize the columns to get the whole timeline to fit on the page.

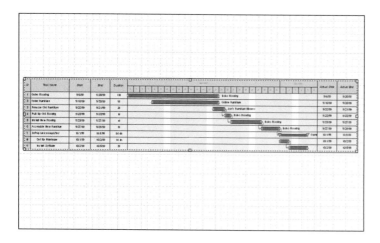

6.

Switch to the Borders and Titles template by clicking on the title bar.

7.

Drag the Border Graduated shape onto the timeline page.

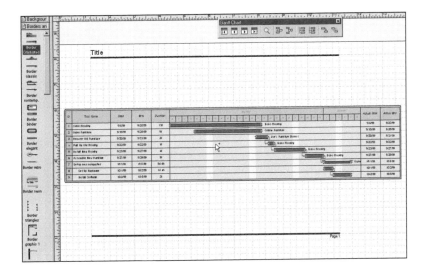

8.

The border automatically resizes to match the page. Double-click on the text Title and enter the title for this diagram: "Office Furniture Installation Timeline".

Save the file, and you're done.

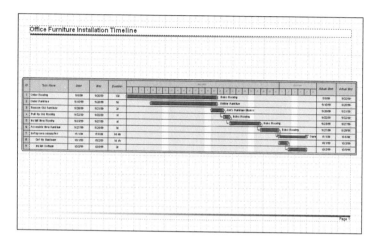

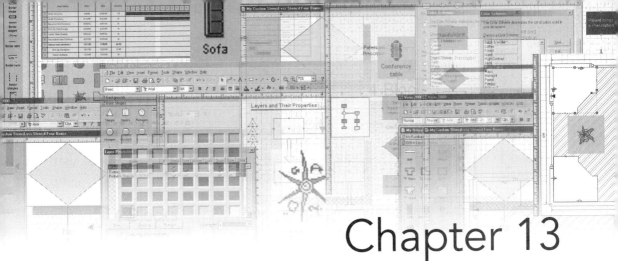

Chapter 13
Adding A Visio Drawing
To Another Document

Project 1: Create a Visio drawing inside another document

Project 2: Insert an existing Visio drawing into another document using embedding and linking

Object Linking And Embedding

As you've seen throughout this book, Visio 2000 can build a wide variety of useful diagrams. One way to use Visio drawings is to print the drawings or save them in a Web-compatible format for posting to a Web site. However, you may also wish to use the Visio drawings as part of a word processing document or a presentation (such as those you can create with Microsoft PowerPoint or Lotus Freelance). This chapter shows you how to use Object Linking and Embedding (OLE) to place your Visio drawing in almost any other type of document. You'll be using Microsoft Word in these projects, but OLE works the same in any type of document.

Project 1: Creating A New Visio Drawing In A Document

Many applications enable you to create a file for another application right inside a document. For example, you can create a Word document that includes a new Visio 2000 drawing.

1.

The first step is to run Microsoft Word and create a new, blank document (although you can insert a new Visio drawing into an existing document as well).

Then, select Insert|Object from the main menu.

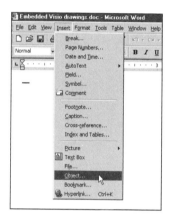

2.

From the Create New tab, scroll down and choose Visio 2000 Drawing.

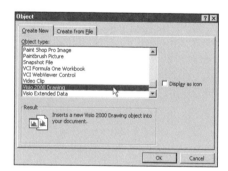

3.

A familiar dialog box appears: the Choose A
Drawing Template dialog box.

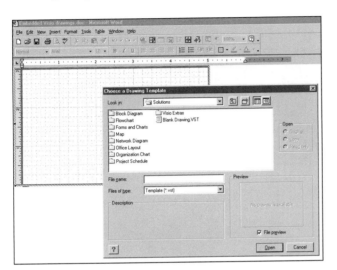

4.

Open the Flowchart folder and choose Basic
Flowchart.

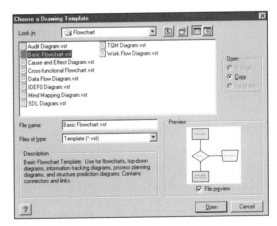

5.

Click on the Open button in the dialog box. A blank Visio diagram appears in the Word document, complete with the stencils you'll need to build the diagram.

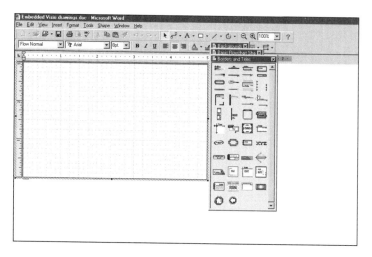

6.

Click on and drag the sizing handle in the lower-right corner of the Visio drawing area to enlarge the drawing. Then, drag the three stencils out of the way by placing them along the right side of the drawing area. Notice that the toolbars and menus visible at the top of the screen are those from Visio; they have replaced the normal Word menus and toolbars.

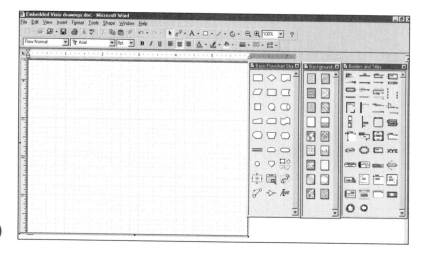

7.

Using the techniques you've already learned, build a flowchart using Visio 2000's tools.

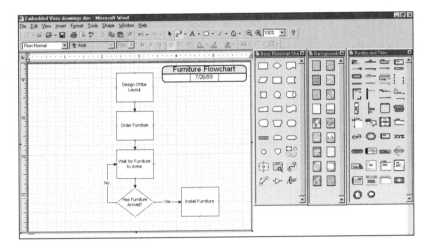

8.

Once you've finished building the diagram, simply click outside the drawing area. The content of the drawing is still visible, but you are now back in Word, with Word's menus and toolbars visible. You can continue creating the Word document using normal techniques.

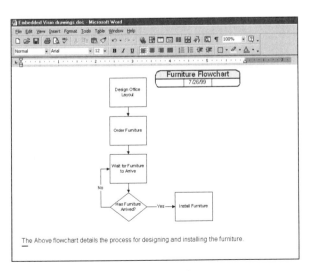

9.

To see the boundary of the diagram in the Word document, click anywhere on the drawing.

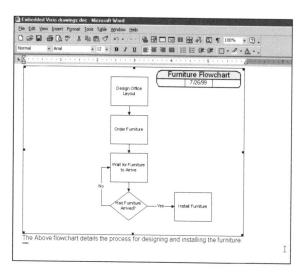

10.

To edit the drawing, double-click on it. This action reopens the diagram so you can make changes to it.

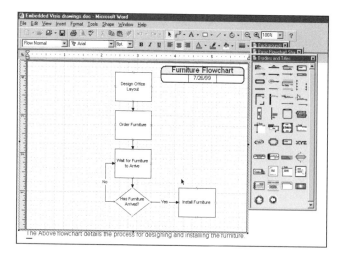

Project 2: Adding An Existing Visio Drawing To A Document

If you have already built a diagram in Visio, as you did in Chapters 10, 11, and 12, you can insert the Visio drawing into a document. The advantage of using existing drawings is that you can use Visio 2000 full-screen, focusing on just building the drawings. Then, when you are ready, you can simply insert the drawings into another document. This is an especially effective method when you're including many Visio 2000 drawings in a PowerPoint or Freelance presentation.

You can insert a Visio diagram into another document using either *embedding* or *linking*. Embedding inserts the drawing into the document. This makes the overall document size larger (which can be a disadvantage), but it simplifies the procedure of giving someone else a copy—you can just give them a copy of the document, and the drawing automatically goes along with it. Another disadvantage of embedding is that, if you have embedded copies of the same drawing in multiple documents and then need to make a change to the drawing, you will have to open each document and make the change.

Linking inserts a pointer to the Visio drawing in the document. If you change the drawing, all documents linked to the drawing will automatically be updated to reflect the change. The document is also smaller because it does *not* contain the drawing. However, if you intend to give a copy of the drawing to someone else, you must remember to give them the file that contains the Visio drawing as well.

Embedding A Drawing

Follow these steps to embed an existing drawing (such as the Office Layout drawing you built in Chapter 10) into a Word document.

1.

Select Insert|Object from the main menu. When the Object dialog box appears, click on the Create From File tab.

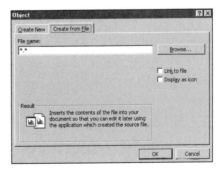

2.

You can either type the file name for the Visio
2000 file into the File Name field, or click on
the Browse button to choose the file from the
Browse dialog box.

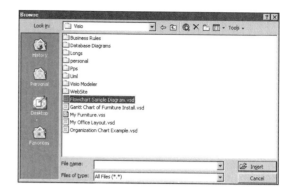

3.

Choose a file (such as My Office Layout.vsd),
click on the Insert button, and then click on
OK in the Object dialog box. The Visio 2000
drawing is inserted into the document.

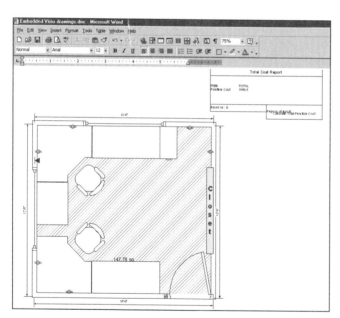

4.

Similar to a new drawing, you can double-click
on the embedded drawing to open it for editing.

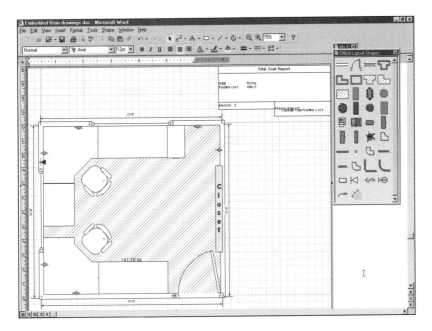

Linking A Drawing

Follow these steps to link an existing drawing (such as the timeline you built in Chapter 12) to
a Word document.

1.

Select Insert|Object from the main menu.
When the Object dialog box appears, click on
the Create From File tab. As before, choose the
file name (this time choose Gantt Chart of
Furniture Install.vsd), and be sure to select the
Link To File checkbox.

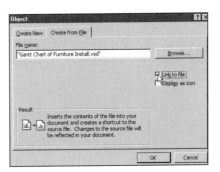

2.

Click on OK to place the linked diagram on the page.

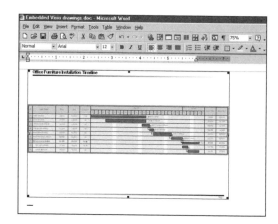

3.

You can edit the resulting diagram by double-clicking on it. However, unlike an embedded drawing, a linked drawing opens in its own Visio window.

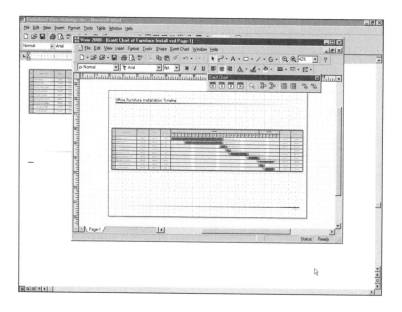

4.

If you make changes without saving, Visio will prompt you to save your changes when you close the Visio drawing. Once you save your changes, the drawing in the document is automatically updated to reflect the changes.

Index

recently used files, 28
reordering pages in, 71
ruler and grid settings, 75–76
sample drawings or starter diagrams, 34
saving, 5, 42–43
shrinking to fit on paper, 272
Diamonds on shapes (vertexes), 54, 55
Dictionaries for spell checker, 29, 134–135
Directories, 29, 43
Displaying. *See* Showing.
Distributing shapes evenly on pages, 100–103
Dividing shapes, 158–162
Docking
    stencils, 46
    toolbars, 23
    windows, 12
Documents. *See* Diagrams.
Double-click behavior of shapes, 167–170
Dragging shapes into diagrams, 48–50
Dragging shapes onto stencils, 190
Drawing area, 5
Drawing drop-down menu, 6
Drawing Explorer window, 172
Drawing master shape icons, 198
Drawing scale, 65–66, 217
Drawing shapes, 5, 7
Drawings. *See* Diagrams.
Duplicating shapes, 7, 50–51, 94–95, 240
Duration of tasks, 266

E

Editable stencils, 190, 235
Editing
    background pages, 84
    custom properties, 138–142
    graphics and clip art, 175–177
    grouped shapes, 109
    inserted diagrams, 280, 283, 284
    master shapes, 193–194
    protecting shapes against edits, 170–172
    shapes, 91, 109, 163, 220–222, 234–241
    styles, 150–152
    text, 58–59, 60, 62
Embedding diagrams into documents, 276–283
Ending dates in Gantt charts, 259, 263, 264, 268

Ending points of lines, 15, 93–94, 171
Ends of lines, shape of, 8, 9, 93
Estimating furniture costs, 242–246
Example drawings, 34
Excel files for organization charts, 248–250

F

Fields
    fixed and variable fields, 143
    in organization charts, 252
File formats for graphics files, 173
File properties, 35
Files. *See* Diagrams.
Fill colors and patterns
    applying to graphics or clip art, 176
    applying to shapes, 8, 92, 228–229
    applying with styles, 147, 149, 150, 151
Fit Curve operation, 162
Fitting diagrams on pages, 65, 271–272
Fixed list fields, 143
Flipping shapes, 105, 177
Floating stencils, 46
Folders, 29, 43
Fonts, 8, 118–119, 121, 126, 128
Footers on pages, 85–86
Foreground colors, 76
Foreground pages, 81–84
Format Painter button, 5, 6
Formatting
    copying formats, 6
    data, 141, 249–250
    graphics or clip art, 176
    menus and tools for, 5, 6, 8–9, 118–120
    styles, 146–152
    Text dialog box, 126–133
    text shortcut menu, 120–121
Fragment operation, 159
Freeform tool, 7
Full screen view, 81
Furniture layout
    adding furniture to rooms, 234–241
    cost estimates for offices, 242–246
    creating stencils for special furniture, 231–233
    reports, 243–246
    room sizes, 216–230

JPEG files, 174
Jumping
    to other pages, 5, 71–73, 169–170
    over connecting lines, 69
    using hyperlinks. *See* Hyperlinks.
Justifying text, 130

K

Keyboard shortcuts. *See* Shortcuts.

L

Labels on reports, 245
Landscape page orientation, 65, 271
Layers, 204. *See also* Background pages.
    active, 205
    assigning shapes to, 208–211
    calculating number of shapes on, 207
    coloring, 209
    creating, 204–207
    deleting, 211–212
    locking, 209
    nonprinting, 205
    numbering shapes on, 157
    reporting shape data for, 144, 243
    visible and invisible, 210
Layout styles for connectors, 67–69
Line jumps over connectors, 69
Lines. *See also* Connecting shapes.
    changing shape outlines, 90–91
    colors and styles, 8, 76, 93–94, 147, 148, 150, 151
    drawing tools, 5, 7
    formatting, 8–9
    on graphics or clip art, 176
    line ends, 8–9, 93
    patterns, 8–9, 90
    starting and ending points, 15, 93–94, 171
    width, 8–9, 90
Lining up shapes, 97–99
Linking. *See also* Hyperlinks.
    diagrams into documents, 281, 283–284
    pages to other pages, 71–73
    tasks in Gantt charts, 265, 266
Listing shapes in reports, 245
Lists, bulleted, 125, 131–132

Locking layers, 209
Locking shapes, 170–172

M

Macros, running, 168
Magnifying drawings, 5, 8, 10–13, 80–81, 88
Manually numbering shapes, 153–154
Margins around text, 131
Master properties, adding, 235
Master shape icons, 191, 192
    editing master shape icons, 197–199
    generating automatically, 193
Master shapes. *See also* Master shape icons.
    copying existing master shapes, 196–197
    creating from scratch, 195–196
    creating from shapes on pages, 190–194
    editing, 193–194
Measurement units, 67
Measuring office rooms, 219–222
Merging shapes. *See* Grouping shapes; Joining or splitting shapes.
Microsoft Clip Gallery, 174
Microsoft Excel files, 248–250
Microsoft PowerPoint Slide Show output, 36
Microsoft Word, 181–182, 276–284
Minimizing windows to title bars, 13
Moving
    assigning shapes to different layers, 208–211
    connected shapes, 54
    connection lines between shapes, 54, 57
    connector points, 7
    graphics or clip art, 175
    guides on pages, 40
    handles on shapes, 56
    independent text blocks, 115
    sending shapes forward or backward, 103–104
    shapes, 53–54
    shapes onto stencils, 191
    stencils on screen, 45–46
    text within shapes, 114
    vertexes on shapes, 55
    zero points on rulers, 37–38, 75, 219
Multiple connections on shape sides, 74
Multiple hyperlinks for shapes, 185–186